"A WOMAN FEARING NOTHING"

THE STORY OF SARAH BRADLEE FULTON: A REVOLUTIONARY WAR HEROINE

Brenda Ely Albus

Copyright © 2014 by Brenda Ely Albus.

All rights reserved.

ISBN: 978-1-312-36585-8

To My Mother

ABOUT THE SPELLING OF NAMES

The preface to the *History of the Bradley Family: with Particular Reference to the Descendants of Nathan Bradley, Of Dorchester, Mass.* by Samuel Bradlee Doggett states: "The name was originally spelled Bradley, the change to Bradlee being made by Samuel Bradlee [father of Sarah Bradlee Fulton]....Family tradition has it that the Bradleys in Dorchester were so numerous that mistakes were made, to obviate which Samuel Bradley changed the final letter to *e*." I have tried to maintain these spellings, using Bradley for the generations before Samuel, and Bradlee for subsequent generations. Quoted materials, of course, retain their original spellings. The eighteenth century seemed little concerned with how a name should be spelled, often using different spellings within the same document. The name Fulton sometimes appears as Fullton.

FOREWORD

It was seeing her dress that first made me want to write about Sarah. It was the oldest dress on display at the DAR Museum in Washington, D.C. in an exhibit which traced the evolution of American wedding dresses since the founding of the country. Made in 1762 for the wedding of my great-great-great-great grandmother, Sarah Bradlee Fulton, it had been donated to the DAR by my grandmother. But for two hundred years it had been a cherished family heirloom, passed down from mother to eldest daughter through five generations.[1] All of these women had lived within a few blocks of Sarah's home in Medford, Massachusetts. The stories about her were part of the history of the town and, like the dress, had been faithfully preserved by her descendants.

Sarah was a heroine of the Revolutionary War. In the years after the war both President George Washington and the Marquis de Lafayette came to her home to pay their respects and to honor her for her courageous acts. Although Medford still pays tribute to her, her brave deeds are now little remembered beyond the confines of her hometown.

1

THE DRESS

The dress is made of deep green silk damask, a remarkable color for the time period, as it was difficult to produce stable green dyes in the eighteenth century.[1] The weave creates a rich pattern of satin and flat finishes. It was costly material, almost certainly imported from England.[2] The colonies in America were meant to provide revenue to the mother country and much of what the colonists bought, particularly luxury items, came from England. Boston, where Sarah Bradlee lived as a young woman, was a primary port of entry for these goods.

Sarah would have gone to a milliner's shop and chosen this splendid fabric and then stood in the shop in her corset while the milliner draped the fabric over her and cut the bodice to an exact fit.

The finished dress was the height of fashion. It had an open-front skirt displaying a contrasting panel, and an open-front bodice into which a "stomacher"—a panel trimmed with costly lace or ribbons—would have been fitted.[3] The back was cut in such a way that it forced her to stand with her shoulders pulled back, and the elbows were sewn with a bend in them, so she would always have her arms slightly curved in front of her.[4] It was to be her wedding dress. The year was 1762, Sarah Bradlee was twenty-two years old and she was going to marry John Fulton. With her head filled with thoughts of marriage and family she would have had no inkling that the events of the next few years would shape her into a woman ready to play her role in the struggle to create a new country.

Sarah must have been stunning in her new green dress. There is no known picture of her, but family tradition holds that she was small and pretty, with dark hair. From the size of her dress it appears that she was about five-feet three-inches tall with delicate shoulders and a small waist. John would have worn the typical groom's clothes of the day: knee breeches, white silk stockings, buckle shoes, a long-skirted coat and perhaps an embroidered waistcoat.

The wedding most likely took place in her parents' home. It was, like all Massachusetts marriages of the time, a civil ceremony. Church weddings with the bride in white, the veil, the wedding march, and the procession of bridesmaids down the aisle—these all came later in American history. The ceremony was performed by the Reverend John Moorhead, the long-time minister of John's family's church, and recorded thus in the records of what is now The Arlington Street Church: "1762 July 25th Were Married John Fulton and Sarah Bradly."[5] After the ceremony they would have celebrated, with family and friends in their best finery, the house decorated with summer flowers and greenery, a sumptuous array of food and, most assuredly, a good rum punch.

John Fulton was a rum distiller. His parents were among the Scotch-Irish immigrants who came to America in the early eighteenth century—Irish Presbyterian dissenters descended from the Scots who had been transplanted to Ireland a hundred years earlier. In Boston their first meeting house was a converted barn on Long Lane (now the corner of Federal and Channing Streets) in the south end of the city. Called "The Church of the Presbyterian Strangers" by a community not overly hospitable to the Scotch-Irish newcomers, it was founded by the Reverend John Moorhead on November 15, 1729. John's parents, John Fulton and Ann Wire (Wier, Wyer), were married by Moorhead on August 3, 1732, and their son, John, was baptized by him on October 21, 1733.[6,7] The Fulton family appears to have made their home on Essex Street in Boston's South End, not far from the Long Lane meeting house. The area had been the center of the distillery business since 1714.[8,9]

2

PURITAN ANCESTORS

Sarah's forbearers were part of the "Great Migration"—those early English Puritans who came to New England in the 1630s seeking to practice a more "pure" form of their religion. They had signed on to be part of the Massachusetts Bay Company, chartered by Charles I in 1629. It was a marriage of convenience. The British government wanted to expand its settlements and create more opportunities for trade. The Puritans hoped to escape the persecution of the Anglican Church and create an ideal Christian community where they could practice a reformed version of their religion, free from any outside control.

They were a stern people who valued hard work, frugality, and civic commitment. Individual needs were subordinate to those of the community. From the pulpit they were admonished that it was "better an innocent and a good man should suffer than order; for that preserves the whole."[1]

They were Calvinists. They believed in predestination and original sin, and they vehemently rejected the papist remnants of the Church of England —its liturgical trappings, its hierarchal structure, and its inability to demand godly living in either its members or its clergy. They recognized only the sacraments of baptism and communion—those in which Christ himself had participated. Marriages were celebrated at home. Funerals were graveside gatherings. There were no prayers for the souls of the dead—their fate had already been determined. There were no days set aside for religious celebrations. Christmas was the same as any other day.[2]

Because they rejected any ecclesiastical hierarchy, the people in each community formed their church by joining together in a covenant that they themselves had written. Each church chose and ordained its own minister.[3] Nevertheless, despite their independent standing, they were in "fellowship" with the other Puritan churches of the Massachusetts Bay. Ministers often preached at each other's churches, either on Sunday or at the Puritan version of entertainment—the Thursday lecture. Members from one church frequently attended the ordination of another church's minister. A congregation troubled by some conflict might ask other churches to send a council of leaders to offer advice in resolving its dispute. This relationship between the Puritan churches came to be called "the Standing Order of the New England Way."[4]

In all it is estimated that there were about 20,000 Puritan immigrants who came to the Massachusetts Bay Colony during the decade before the beginnings of the English Civil War—a migration that stopped abruptly when the English Puritans had reason to hope for change at home. Thus, those who trace their ancestry back to the Massachusetts Puritans find themselves descended from this small number of people—mostly middle class, mostly literate, and mostly having immigrated as a family group.[5]

Sarah's Puritan ancestors settled in Dorchester, a farming and fishing village about five miles south of Boston. The first of these settlers left England aboard the *Mary and John* on March 20, 1630, one of eighteen ships that arrived in Massachusetts that year. They had formed their church and chosen their ministers before they set sail. However by 1636 the majority of these people had moved to Connecticut. This migration was in large part prompted by the promise of more fertile land, but it may also have had something to do with the growing controversy within the Massachusetts Bay Colony over who could be admitted to the church.[6]

There was little question about the first Massachusetts Bay colonists' claims to church membership. They were united by their experiences of persecution in England and their willingness to risk all in order to establish a godly society in this far-away wilderness. But in the same year that the Dorchester people moved to Connecticut, the Massachusetts Bay Colony established a rigid procedure for the founding of a new church and the admitting of new members. The "gathering" of a church began with at least seven men who were able to demonstrate their knowledge of Calvinist doctrine, achievement of a godly life, and evidence of a personal spiritual regeneration. A council made up of ministers from nearby churches and civil magistrates of the colony had to be present to verify the proceedings.[7] Once a church was established, new members had to undergo the same stern examination by the elders. Also, from this time on, the Massachusetts Colony granted freemanship—the right to vote and to hold public office—only to men who had attained church membership.

Dorchester, needing to reestablish its church, may have been the first congregation to fall under these new requirements. The candidates and their prospective minister, Richard Mather, who had arrived in Boston the year before, met with the council on April 1, 1636. Their confession of faith was deemed acceptable, but only Mather and one other man were found able to give satisfactory evidence of their spiritual experience. Governor Winthrop, who recorded the meeting in his journal, writes that "they had builded their comfort of salvation on unsound ground." Presumably having been instructed by Mather, the other candidates must have eventually been approved by the council, for the Dorchester church was founded on August 23, 1636.[8] The existing church records date from that time.

Sarah's earliest recorded ancestor in Dorchester was Thomas Andrews (Andrewes, Andrus), her maternal great-great grandfather. He was a mason.[9] He must have been one of the early settlers who chose not to move to Connecticut, for the town records show him to have been awarded "2 acres of ground betwixt Mr. Hathornes house and the high way from Roxbury" on November 22, 1634.[10] He shortly built a house on that land, and on December 17, 1635 the town allotted him another three acres "next his house neere Mr. Hathornes."[11] In a further division of land in 1637 he was awarded another five-plus acres of outlying town land.[12]

Thomas's name next appears among the signers of a document of 1641 regarding the funding of the town school[13]—a matter of great importance to the community. The Puritan religion was centered on the authority of the Holy Scriptures and the belief that the path to salvation for each individual was through the knowledge and understanding of the Bible. Thus it was vital that children be taught to read. Within its first ten years the Massachusetts Bay Colony passed laws mandating the establishment of a school in any community of more than fifty families. The early town records throughout New England reflect this concern.

Early Dorchester historians maintain that theirs was the first public school—that is, paid for by a direct tax on the town's people—in the American colonies. Quite extraordinarily these first public records in Dorchester even make mention of "whether maydes shall be taught with the boys or not."[14] Yet the issue seems never to have been mentioned again and the schools so established were for boys. Little girls were allowed only the limited education provided by the local dame-school —a school for very young girls and boys, taught in a neighbor woman's home. In the dame-school the children used a horn book—a piece of heavy paper on which was printed the alphabet and the Lord's Prayer, covered over with a thin piece of horn to keep it from being soiled—to learn their letters. Then they proceeded to learn to read from the New England Primer, with its repeated emphasis on sin and death: "In Adam's fall, We sinned all. Thy life to mend, God's Book attend." From there the boys could move on to grammar school and proceed to read through the Psalter, the New Testament, and finally the complete Bible. Those with the aptitude and the means might eventually enroll in Harvard, established in 1636 as a training ground for ministers and teachers. Boston would have no town-supported schooling for girls until after the Revolutionary War.[15]

Sarah's great-great grandfather on her father's side, Richard Evans, whose daughter, Mary, married Nathan Bradley in 1666, is named on a list of immigrants who arrived about the same time as Richard Mather.[16,17] Richard Evans is recorded as having taken the Freeman's oath in 1643, and both he (Richard Eavins) and Goody Eavens are recorded as "taking hold of the covent" that same year.[18]

Nathan Bradley's name first appears in the Dorchester town records in 1667, where he is recorded as owning two acres of the "Great Lots."[19] He must have been poor, because the town selectmen granted his petition of 1673 for liberty to sell cider at retail: "considering his low condition...with the ap'bation of the Court he observeing to keepe good order in soe doeing and attending the law therin."[20] On the same day it was "granted to Nathan Bradley liberty to take two or three load of timber off from the 500 acres towards the building him a hous."[21] Being licensed to sell cider, Nathan would have built his house in the center of the village.

In 1680, having taken the Oath of Allegiance in 1679, he was appointed sexton of the newly-built meeting house, a job he held for several years. He was to "ring the bell, cleanse the meeting house, and to carry water for baptism...." While the bell stood on the hill, Mr. Bradley was to have 'after four pounds a year; and after the bell is brought to the meetinghouse L3 10s."[22] This new meeting house, begun in 1676, had been built by a member of the congregation—one Isaac Royal.[23] Many years later another Isaac Royall in another Massachusetts town would play a part in this story.

The meeting house was a rude square building, two stories high, with a bell tower in the center. Similar style meeting houses were built all over Massachusetts at the time. The interiors were plain, with rows of backless benches facing a raised pulpit. There was no heat, partly because the building was also used to store the town's supply of powder.[24] A Sunday thunderstorm could send everyone scurrying out of the building.

The Sabbath was completely given over to worship. Beginning with family prayers on Saturday night, the day was to be kept holy with no work or play allowed. Massachusetts law required that everyone attend church.

The Bradley family and their neighbors may have set out for church all dressed in black, but this was more likely true for the ruling elders and others of high rank— those seen in paintings of the period. Most wore "sadd colors," russet and philly mort (from the French *feuille morte*, or *dead leaf*) being the most common—colors that did not show the dirt.[25] Sumptuary laws gave them little freedom to adorn their garments. As early as 1639 the court directed that "Whereas there is much complaint of the excessive wearing of lace, and other superfluities tending to little use or benefit, but to the nourishing of pride and exhausting of mens estates, and also of evile example to others, it is therefore ordered...that henceforward no person whatsoever shall presume to sell or buy...any manner of lace...And that hearafter no garment shalbee made with short sleeves, whereby the nakedness of the arme may bee discovered...And that hearafter no person whatsoever shall make any garment for weomen...with sleeves more than halfe an elle wide." Also prohibited were "Great breches, knots of ryban, broad shoulder bands, and rayles, silk rases, double ruffes, and cuffes."[26]

Once inside the meeting house "the seating of the congregation was done with a certain deference to rank and influence. In a little enclosure under the pulpit sat the elders and deacons [facing the rest of the congregation]...in the first seat on the right sat the selectmen. In the other seats, according to age and rank came the other town officials and after them farmers and tradesmen." Men and women were seated on opposite sides of the church. The young people and children were consigned to the back of the room and "taxed to the utmost the tithing-men, who sought with their long poles and attached foxtails to keep the unruly suppressed and the sleepy ones awake."[27]

The seating lists for the Dorchester meeting house for the years 1693 and 1698 still exist. In 1698 Thomas Andrews Jr. was seated in "the 3rd seat below" and Nathan Bradley Sr. in the "6th seat below." Their wives occupied comparable seats on the women's side. Isaac and William Ryolls and their wives were seated in the same rows as Thomas Andrews and his wife.[28]

The congregation would rise in respect as the minister, clad in his black academic robe, entered the room, climbed the stairs of the pulpit and stood to face them, a large hour-glass at his side.[29] A sermon could last two hours or more, and, in general, was crafted to appeal more to the listener's intellect than to his emotions. "It began with a powerful and usually puzzling scrap of Scripture which was relentlessly analyzed and ramified in a prolonged discussion called 'the finding out'."[30] People often took notes as an aid to further their study.

Prayers could last over an hour. The congregation stood during the prayer. Kneeling was out of the question; the first generation of Puritans didn't even bow their heads or close their eyes.[31] At the end of the service they sang a psalm. With no instruments and few hymn books to follow, one member of the group would begin to line the song, choosing one of four or five frequently used tunes, but within a line or two everyone was singing "as best pleased himself...a medley of confused and disorderly noises" from which they apparently derived great pleasure.[32] The service completed, the congregation would return in the afternoon and do it all again.

As the first generation of Puritan children grew to adulthood new questions about church membership arose. Grown children of church members, having been baptized as babies, were required to undergo the same examination of their experience of spiritual regeneration as any other prospective candidate. Such an experience, however much desired and prayed for, might not be realized until late in life—or perhaps never. Were their children to be denied baptism?[33] At a synod of 1657 it was decided that if a person born and baptized in the church did not receive faith he could still be a member and have his children baptized. To do so he must lead a life free of scandal, learn and profess the doctrines of Christianity, and "own the covenant"—that is, make a voluntary submission to God and his church. Termed the "Halfway Covenant," such a member was not admitted to the communion table.[34]

Thus, within one generation, the New England Puritan church found itself unable to realize the vision of those first immigrants—the establishment of a community of "visible saints" who believed themselves chosen for salvation. Their children had shown themselves less inclined to intense religious experiences. New immigrants were apt to be more intent on commercial pursuits. The decisive blow came with the English government's recharter of the Massachusetts Bay Colony in 1691. A royal governor, who immediately set about building himself an Anglican church, was installed in Boston. The new charter required religious toleration and ended the religious requirement for suffrage. But even in its less than perfect form the Puritan church still defined New England life.

3

CHILDHOOD

Sarah was born a little more than 100 years after the settlement of Dorchester. Her birth is entered in the records of the church: "Sarah ye Daughter of Samuel and Mary Bradley, was Born Decr 24th 1740."[1] Her parents were in covenant with the church, but apparently not in full communion. That year "the fall of snow was unusually heavy and the cold so bitter that even Dorchester Bay was solidly frozen."[2] Most likely Sarah was carried out into the raw air the very next Sunday to be baptized by Rev. Jonathan Bowman in the old meeting house that Isaac Royal had built. Inside it was almost as cold as outside, and the ice had to be broken off the top of the baptismal water before it could be administered. This meeting house, where the first Nathan Bradley had served as sexton, was now almost sixty years old. Sarah's childhood memories would mostly be of the fine new meeting house, with a tower and steeple, which was built three years later.

  Childhood was not to be idled away, and one can imagine little Sarah, perhaps as young as three, holding her sister Mary's hand and setting off to dame-school. She would have carried her horn book and, soon, her stern New England Primer. Then, while the little boys went off to continue their education, Sarah and the other little girls may have stayed longer in the dame-school, practicing their reading and learning to stitch their letters. Beyond this her education would have been at home.

To manage a home and family in colonial times was a formidable task. Preparing food meant not just cooking it, but growing, processing, and preserving it. Livestock needed tending. Keeping one's family in clothes required spinning, weaving and sewing—and then washing and mending. Knitting sat on the table, ready to be picked up in a rare moment of inactivity. Tending sick children called for knowledge of herbs and whatever limited medicines were available. Sarah, as the fifth of twelve children, would have been well-practiced in tending babies and little children long before she had a family of her own. Only one of her siblings, baby Daniel, did not survive infancy. Quite remarkably, all the others lived well into their adult years.

Dorchester was a pretty village, with hills and valleys sloping down to its own ample harbor. The Massachusetts waters were rich with fish, and fishing, particularly cod fishing, was a vital industry. Sarah's father was a fisherman, as were some of his brothers[3]—rugged men who sailed out day after day into the rough and unforgiving Atlantic waters. The village was sprinkled with orchards and gardens and from the high ground one could see the whole of Boston Harbor. How beautiful for a little girl to scramble up a hill on a bright spring day, breathe in the untainted air, and look out on the sparkling water and a landscape unspoiled by steel and concrete.

Still there were troublesome events too, and the children, listening to the grownup conversations, must have worried and wondered about the ways of the world. The ongoing wars between England and France sometimes reached the colonies. In 1745 Massachusetts raised a large militia to attack the French at Nova Scotia and capture the fort at Louisburg. It was a great victory. However many of the soldiers died of a fever soon after, and a number of men from Dorchester were among them. The following year the French set out to attack Boston in retaliation. Frantic defense measures were set up in the harbor, and the people were in a great state of panic.[4] Sarah's father and her uncles, Jonathan and Josiah, may have been among those enlisted to defend the city[5], but as the French fleet neared the harbor a huge storm suddenly blew up, disabling most of the French ships and forcing them to abandon their assault. When the peace between Britain and France was signed two years later the colonists felt themselves betrayed. Louisburg was given back to the French. The British government seemed to have given little thought to Massachusetts' great sacrifices.

The royal government showed its disregard for the rights of the colonists in other ways. In 1747, when their navy had needed more sailors, they had begun impressing men right off the streets of Boston. Men just like Sarah's father had been kidnapped in broad daylight and forced into service. The citizens responded with prolonged rioting. In spite of their regard for an orderly society, or perhaps because of it, grownups sometimes took matters into their own hands. Perhaps it was sometimes necessary to break the rules.

These same years were also marred by turmoil in the church. Sarah had been born in the year of "The Great Awakening"—the year that the English revivalist preacher, the Reverend George Whitefield, arrived in Boston. The Puritan religion, while still the paramount force in colonial life, had been tempered by many outside influences, most notably the great rationalists' writings coming out of England—the Enlightenment. The Great Awakening was a reaction to this more rational approach to religion. The founder of the movement in New England was the Reverend Jonathan Edwards of the inland Massachusetts town of Northampton. He preached the necessity of an emotional religious conversion, a "born again" experience in which the grace of God changed one's heart. Other ministers soon took up his evangelical style.

The arrival of George Whitefield served to fan these flames. Educated at Oxford and ordained by the Church of England, he was a highly charismatic preacher who excited the religious fervor of many of the people who flocked to hear him preach. He must have been an extraordinary speaker. Even such a religious skeptic as Benjamin Franklin spoke well of him, and was persuaded to empty his pockets into the collection basket on at least one occasion after hearing him speak.[6] Whitefield's final sermon, delivered on the Boston Common, was attended by more than 23,000 people—more than the entire population of the city.[7]

Yet there were many, particularly many of the established clergy, who disliked the extravagance of Whitefield's, and his followers', preaching. They found the emphasis on an emotional religious experience an insult to their more ordered approach to scripture, and they resented the often-uninvited intrusion of these preachers into the life of their community. "There were troublesome times among clergy and laity for a long time after Mr. Whitfield's visit, the old order of things being broken in upon and many churches filled with bickering and division."[8]

Dorchester was one of those congregations to be troubled. The controversy festered for several years and by 1747 had become so intense that a council had to be called. Leaders from nearby churches were sent to the village and for four days "sat chiefly at the meeting-house, where there was a Publick Hearing and a great throng of People, many from other Towns."[9] The whole affair was a great source of worry and expense.

The divisions that grew out of the Great Awakening marked the beginning of the end of the Standing Order of the New England Puritan churches. It would take many years, but within Sarah's lifetime the church would split into evangelical and rationalistic factions in what became known as the Unitarian Controversy.[10]

Only six years old, Sarah would have been aware of the turmoil going on in her little town, and, although she wouldn't have understood all that was happening, it must have implanted in her young mind the knowledge that religion could be viewed in more than one way.

4

BOSTON BEFORE THE WAR

In 1750 Sarah's grandfather Nathan Bradley was found floating in the water, apparently having fallen out of his canoe and drowned.[1] Years later, alone in her own small boat on the Charles River, this memory would be with Sarah as she struggled to carry out her patriotic mission.

Sarah's father was elected to be Dorchester's constable in 1753, but someone else had to complete his term of office because the family moved to Boston during that year.[2] Sarah's grandmother, Lydia Bradley, had died little more than a year after her husband. Perhaps the death of the grandparents prompted this move. Or perhaps the oldest son, Samuel, then twenty-two years old, had already moved to Boston and the rest of the family decided to follow him. Samuel was a housewright (house carpenter), and soon became an established member of the Boston community. In 1760 he was chosen to be one of Boston's twelve constables,[3] and by 1762 he and his wife Agnes were able to purchase their own house on Essex Street.[4] Whatever the reason, the Bradlees packed family and possessions into carts and drove across the narrow neck of land that led into Boston. It was a bleak entry, past an old windmill and the gallows and through the town gate.

Except for the thin spit of land at the south end connecting it to the mainland, Boston in the mid- to late-eighteenth century was an island. During a stormy high tide the sea could sweep away even this connection. Beyond the neck the land widened out to an irregular shape of land with several sizable hills. The most notable was the tall three-peaked mountain, which dominated the western center of the island, and it was for this that the first settlers had called Boston "Trimountain." To the west the Charles River separated the city from the rest of Massachusetts. To the east was the town harbor—the lifeblood of Boston—and most of the town was nestled between the harbor and the three hills of the "Trimountain."

Were a traveler from the eighteenth century to return to the island of Manhattan today, he would still recognize the shape of the land. The same traveler coming to Boston would find the topography of this city unrecognizable. In the course of the nineteenth and twentieth centuries the hills of Boston were shorn away and used to fill in the harbors until the city, today triple its original size, became an almost flat extension of the mainland. The area around Beacon Hill, much reduced from its original heights, is all that remains of the old "Trimountain," although its memory lingers in the name of Tremont Street.

A visitor from England, an Anglican clergyman, traveling in the colonies in 1759, describes Boston thus: "Boston, the metropolis of Massachusetts-Bay, in New England, is one of the largest and most flourishing towns in North America. It is situated upon a peninsula...at the bottom of a spacious and noble harbor, defended from the sea by a number of small islands. The length of it is nearly two miles, and the breadth of it half a one; and it is supposed to contain 3000 houses, and 18 or 20 thousand inhabitants. At the entrance of the harbor stands a very good light-house; and upon an island, about a league from the town, a considerable castle (Castle William), mounting near 150 cannon....

The chief public buildings are three churches [by which he means Anglican churches—King's Chapel, Christ Church (Old North), and Trinity (then on the corner of Summer and Hawley Streets, not far from where Sarah lived)], thirteen or fourteen meeting-houses, the governor's palace [Province House], the court-house [Old State House] or exchange, Faneuils-hall, a linen-manufacturing-house, a work-house, a bridewell, a public granary, and a very fine wharf, at least half a mile long, undertaken at the expense of a number of private gentlemen for the advantage of unloading and loading vessels."[5]

This "unloading and loading" of vessels was central to the life of Boston, with the rum trade as well as fishing and ship building providing much of the wealth of the city. Long Wharf, to which the eighteenth-century visitor refers, could accommodate some thirty ships, but the entire eastern side of the island was jutted with smaller wharves. The rocks and islands at the mouth of the harbor provided for a narrow and well-guarded entry, but once inside there was room for many ships.

From the head of Long Wharf, King Street led west to the Town House (today the Old State House), the seat of the colonial government. It was there that the royal governor met with his Council and the House of Representatives. The governor, lieutenant governor, and some of the other colonial officials were appointed by the King, but the members of the House of Representatives were elected by the people of Massachusetts. They voted the taxes to be levied on the colonists, and the salaries to be paid to the governor and other royal appointees. A little to the north of the Town House was Faneuil Hall, which housed a large open market on the ground floor and a meeting hall on the floor above. The town meetings were held there, as were the frequent meetings of the selectmen, elected to oversee the governing of the city.

The center of the town was a maze of narrow, winding streets, crowded with houses and shops. Most of the buildings were made of wood, making fire an ever-present danger, and Sarah would have remembered with horror the Great Fire that had destroyed so much of the city just two years before she was married. On the wider streets, some paved with stones, there were fine brick buildings, and the city's wealthiest citizens had magnificent homes. Mr. Hancock's mansion, surrounded by gardens and orchards, was the grandest home in Boston. One of Massachusetts' most successful shipping merchants, he had inherited a great fortune from his uncle and was now reputed to be the richest man in the colony. The privileged few such as John Hancock might travel about town in an elegant coach. Everyone else vied with the carts and various four-footed beasts for the least muddy parts of the streets.

Many of the artisans had their shops in the front of their homes. The signs outside had pictures on them, so people who couldn't read would know what kind of shop it was. One of them would have been the milliner's shop where Sarah had had her wedding dress made. Paul Revere's silver shop was at the north end of town. There he fashioned exquisite silver tea sets and fine silver dinnerware, and also buttons and buckles and other items made from less precious metals.

The print shops were busy turning out newspapers and handbills and advertisements of all kinds. Benjamin Franklin had begun his career as a printer there. The newspaper had become increasingly more important in colonial America, and Boston was at the center of its development. In 1722 there were eight print shops in the American colonies—five of them being in Boston. The Puritan belief in the importance of reading the scriptures had produced an exceptionally literate public, now more and more open to new ideas.

By 1760 literacy in Massachusetts—the ability to read, but not necessarily to write—exceeded seventy-five percent.[6]

The center of town was crowded and noisy: the clatter of hooves, the rumble of carts going back and forth to the wharves, the calls of the street vendors, the town crier—a kind of walking newscaster—calling out the happenings of the day. "Lost boy, lost boy!" one might have heard as the crier approached, ringing his bell and giving out a description of the unfortunate child.[7] More often it was an item of news brought by a ship just arrived in port. And everywhere there were the bells —bells that pealed in celebration or tolled in mourning, Sunday morning bells that called the people to meeting, evening bells that sent them home at curfew and, most frightening, bells that called the people out in alarm for a fire or some other disaster.

The Bradlees settled a little away from the center of town, on Auchmuty Street, in Boston's South End. They were part of the working class—people who worked at a trade—then referred to as mechanics. Sarah's father was a fisherman and a weaver. Like his older brother, Nathaniel would become a housewright. Thomas would become a cordwainer, and Josiah, a tinplate worker. Only David, who made his living as a wine merchant, would rise in social status enough to eventually be referred to as a "gentleman." The family probably rented their home on Auchmuty Street—the name given at that time to the portion of Essex Street between Short and South Streets. It bordered the South Cove, in the heart of the distillery district, and was lined with wharves and stillhouses. John Fulton, then twenty years old, probably worked at one of these distilleries.

One might imagine the distillery district to have been in the seediest part of town, but it seems rather to have been in the prettiest. The South End "was very like a large village, for it was in a great measure devoted to gardens, residences, and the large houses of the rich and fashionable."[8] The Royal Governor lived in a house on Winter Street. The north side of Essex Street was mostly open land. The wealthy John Rowe bought property there in 1764 and built a fine new house, using most of the land for raising hay and vegetables and pasturing sheep and cattle.[9] Going east on Essex Street a few blocks, the wide intersection with Orange Street was called Hanover Square, also referred to as "the elm neighborhood" because of the magnificent elm trees that stood there.[10]

Orange Street, earlier called "The High Waye to Roxberrie"[11], was the road that ran along the neck—the only road that linked Boston to the mainland. Hanover Square must have been a convenient stopping point for travelers, as the area became a favorite place for taverns. The busy traffic on Orange Street also made it a logical place for shops. Sarah's mother may have had a shop there. The Selectmen's Minutes of August 4, 1768—one month after Samuel's death—record Mary Bradley as approved for a license as retailer of strong drink "at her shop near Mr. Kneelands, South End".[12] Kneeland Street, where Mr. Kneeland lived at that time, extended from the South Cove out to Orange Street a few streets below Hanover Square. A map of 1769 shows several buildings clustered on Orange Street at the corner of Kneeland Street. One of these could have been Mary's shop. Perhaps she sold Samuel's woven goods there and then converted the shop to a tavern after he died.

The next street west of Orange Street was Common Street (a continuation of Tremont Street), and beyond it was the Common, a large open area sloping down to the marshes at the edge of the Charles River. In the English tradition, it was an area set aside for the common use of the townspeople—particularly as a place for grazing cattle and holding military exercises. By the time Sarah came to Boston, Tremont Street, where it bordered the Common, was a tree-lined pedestrian mall. It was a favorite place for people to promenade.

On the edge of the Common, near the corner of West Street, was the South Writing School—one of Boston's free schools. Sarah's baby brother, Josiah, went to school there when he was older. His name is included in a list of students of 1768, as is that of Gershom Spear, who later married Sarah's youngest sister, Elizabeth.[13] Perhaps some of Sarah's other brothers went to school there too. By that time the traditional Latin grammar schools mostly served the needs of students preparing for the ministry or law. The writing schools, which favored a business education over a classical one, attracted many more students.[14] They taught students to write with exquisite penmanship and they also taught mathematics, particularly as it applied to bookkeeping.[15] In 1755 there were 216 boys enrolled at the South Writing School.[16] It had opened in 1720, and it is likely that John Fulton had attended this same school. For at least some of his career he was the bookkeeper for the distillery where he worked. An article in the Medford Historical Register describes a small receipt written by John many years later as being in "excellent script."[17]

To the east of the Bradlee home, "the extreme point beyond Essex, South, and Federal Streets was called 'Windmill Point.'"[18] Henry Knox, famous in the Revolutionary War for leading a regiment that dragged fifty-nine heavy guns from Ticonderoga to Boston during the winter of 1775-76, was born in this little corner of Boston in 1750, in a house on Sea and Essex Streets.[19] His parents were part of Reverend Morehead's Long

Lane congregation and John would have known them from childhood.[20]

On the other side of Windmill Point, Samuel Adams lived in a somewhat unkempt house on Purchase Street that looked out over the South Harbor. There was a malt house on the property from which he ran a none-too-profitable family brewing business. Adams' father had built the house in 1712 and soon after he and thirteen other men built the New South Meeting House nearby. It sat at the juncture of Pond and Summer Streets, just north of Auchmuty Street. "There was not a more beautiful site for a church in Boston."—it being "high and level, with an unobstructed outlook over the harbor."[21]

The Bradlees joined the New South Meeting House. Their minister, the Reverend Samuel Checkley, whose daughter had married Sam Adams, was a moderate Calvinist. Like so many of the Boston clergy he used his pulpit to express his support for the rights of the colony.[22] Sarah's oldest sister, Lydia, was married by the Rev. Checkley to James Collings (Collins) on Nov 22, 1753 and the newest member of the family, baby Josiah, was baptized at New South the following March—the "son of Samuel and Mary Bradley, in Covenant at Dorchester."[23] It must have been an emotional decision to name this baby Josiah, for his namesake was one of Samuel's younger brothers who had died just two months earlier. He and his brother Jonathan had gone out fishing from Dorchester on a stormy January day and had never returned. Once again the harsh New England sea had claimed some of Sarah's family, a fact she would well remember nearly a quarter of a century later when she was the one to brave the tidal waters around Boston.

Three years later Samuel and Mary's last child, Elizabeth, was baptized at New South,[24] and a month later their first grandchild, the son of Lydia and James Collings, was baptized there too. In time Sarah and John would become part of the New South congregation, as would the families of three of her siblings (David, Nathaniel and Margaret Lloyd). Others in the congregation would, in years to come, be linked with members of Sarah's family.

So much had changed since the beginnings of the Massachusetts Bay Colony. The rigid Puritan religion no longer held absolute sway. The commerce of the busy shipping harbor brought new inhabitants—many of them of dubious religious persuasion. Those same ships had brought a luxury of goods to the people of New England that the founders would never have imagined. Sarah's wedding finery is evidence enough that the old admonitions against lace and ribbons and such no longer applied.

The most conservative Puritan clergy no longer controlled Harvard. Influenced by the new ideas of science and rational thought, it was graduating ministers and teachers of more moderate theology. Perhaps it was not God's wrath that brought storms and pestilence. Perhaps there were more reasoned explanations. The emphasis on predestination and the depravity of man had begun to give way to a more enlightened religion. The controversies that had arisen over Whitefield's preaching had opened the door for discussion of new ways of thinking, and some of the Boston clergy were in the vanguard of these changes. One of the first to speak out against the rigidity of the Calvinist doctrine was the Reverend Jonathan Mayhew, the pastor at the West Church, where Sarah's brother Samuel was a member. It is an indication of the evolving theology that when the still young Jonathan Mayhew died in 1766, Charles Chauncy, perhaps Boston's most noted liberal clergyman, said a prayer at the funeral. It is said to have been the first prayer ever invoked at a funeral in Boston.[25]

Nevertheless the church was still the defining factor in colonial life. Its precepts shaped the culture of the community. Its pastors were the most respected members of society. The Sabbath was for worship, and woe to anyone who did not attend services. No work or leisure activities were allowed. One could not even stroll down the street. But for six days of the week Boston was a hive of activity and Sarah grew from a girl to a young woman in this bustling New England metropolis.

5

EARLY YEARS OF MARRIAGE

Sarah and John must have enjoyed strolling along the tree-lined mall on a summer evening. To the west, across the Common, with the sun setting beyond the Charles River, they could admire John Hancock's grand home. To the east was the view of the town punctuated by its many church spires and, beyond, by the many masts of the ships lying in harbor. Perhaps John proposed to Sarah on such an evening's walk.

There was much to look forward to as the couple planned their life together. Boston, although no longer the largest city in the colonies, was a major port city. The French and Indian War, which had claimed the lives of a disproportionate number of Massachusetts' men, was finally over. England's victory in that phase of her lengthy war with France meant that the Atlantic waters were again safe for shipping and fishing. Young King George III had ascended to the throne, and in spite of their recurring dissatisfactions with the royal government, the colonists were proud Englishmen who held their king in great esteem. However the many years of war with France had left England with a large debt and the need to keep troops in the colonies to protect what she had won there. The colonies, Parliament said, should help pay for these expenses.

The conflict began with molasses, and as distillers the Fultons would have been in the thick of it from the beginning. The sweet brown goo was an inexpensive form of sugar. It was a staple of the colonial kitchen, but it was also used for making rum, and rum was a vital part of the Massachusetts economy. The colonists drank a good bit of the rum they produced, but the greater part of it was shipped to Africa where it was sold or traded for African slaves. The slaves were taken to the West Indies where they were sold and the money used to buy goods from the West Indies, particularly molasses. The molasses was then shipped back to the colonies—much of it to Boston—and used to make more rum. Slavery was not only a sin of the South, it was a part of the northern economy too, just not so observably.

Since New England imported molasses directly from the French West Indies, Parliament had years earlier imposed a tariff on it. But the colonies had ignored the law and had been smuggling most of their molasses into America. One way or another, customs officials could usually be persuaded to look the other way. Now, as the Crown resolved to replenish its coffers, it also wanted to tighten its control over the colonies and it set its sights first on New England's trade revenues. In 1764 the old molasses tariff laws were replaced by the Sugar Act, which placed a tax on molasses and other goods coming from non-British ports. This time Parliament intended it to be enforced.

Already struggling under a post-war depression, the merchants protested that the fees would ruin them, and none would have felt this tax more personally than the rum distillers. Beyond the immediate monetary impact, some argued that while the Crown might have the right to impose tariffs for the purpose of regulating trade with foreign countries, it did not have the right to impose a direct tax solely for the purpose of raising revenue. Revenue taxes had always been voted on by the elected representatives here in America. To do otherwise was a violation of their rights as British citizens. Having allowed the colonists a great degree of freedom in the past, Parliament would find it difficult to take back what it had already given away.

Then, to compound the city's distress, Boston was hit with a devastating outbreak of smallpox. By the end of June, 699 people had contracted the fearful disease, and 124 had died.[1] Shops and markets were closed for weeks. Sarah must have watched with growing dread as more and more red flags appeared, marking the homes where the contagion had struck, and guards were posted to make sure no one entered or left these properties. At night she would have heard the carts going by, and known they were carrying the dead to be buried in the middle of the night, when there was less chance of others coming in contact with the infected bodies. Some people chose to be inoculated, but vaccination itself was dangerous, so it was a difficult decision.

Sarah gave birth to her first child during that terrible epidemic. Little Sarah Lloyd was born on May 20, 1764, during the height of the contagion. It was July 29 before they dared take her to New South to be baptized.[2] John Fulton was admitted to the church on the same day. A year and a half later, December 15, 1765, Sarah and John's first son, John Andrews, was born. By the spring of 1772 they had three more girls—Ann Wier, born December 23, 1767, Mary, born February 10, 1770, and Lydia, born April 22, 1772. All were baptized at New South and all were named for parents, grandparents or great grandparents.[3]

Caring for her growing family, Sarah may well have recited the poems of Mother Goose to her little ones. Not far away, on Winter Street, was the home of the Vergoose family. A Boston legend says that this had been the home of Elizabeth Vergoose, whose son-in-law, the publisher of the Boston Evening Post, had collected his mother-in-law's songs and stories and published them in his paper. Books of all sorts must have been of some importance in Sarah's life. Many years later, one of Sarah's nephews wrote that before his grandmother (Sarah's mother) died, "She gave to me a book for a parting present, to remember her." This nephew became a bookseller.[4] Sarah's children would have had a wider array of books to grow up with than had been available to their mother. A new genre had appeared in London in the 1740s when John Newbery began publishing books written for children's reading pleasure. By the 1760s such books had made their way to Boston. Newbery's books, rather than focusing on the attainment of salvation, frequently extolled the virtue of reading as a path to achieving happiness and, perhaps, wealth in life.

Although the New England Primer, with its constant references to sin and death was still in use, books designed to make learning to read a more pleasant experience were increasingly available. Spelling books—aids to reading that taught children to sound out words syllable by syllable—had been in existence for many years, but only began to be used extensively in the 1750s. They were the first chink in the religious armor of reading instruction. A new spelling book, widely available in Boston after 1750, makes a sharp contrast to the New England Primer. *The Child's New Play-Thing, Being a Spelling-book intended to make the Learning to read a Diversion instead of a Task* begins: "A apple-pye, B bit it, C cut it, D divided it, E eat it."[5]

6

THE LIBERTY TREE

Today, in the area around Essex Street, there is almost nothing remaining of the neighborhood where John and Sarah raised their young family. The quaint homes and gardens and orchards have been replaced by nondescript city buildings. South Cove with its many stillhouse wharves has been filled in to create more city streets. The graceful shade trees that arched over the village streets are long gone—including the elms at the corner of Essex and Orange Streets. It was under one of these magnificent trees, just a short walk from Sarah's house, that the seeds of the revolution were sown. In a society where the "better sort" ran the government, it was there that the working class citizens—Sarah among them—found their voice. Given what is known of the Bradlee family's political views, they must have played a significant part in the events that took place there.

By the beginning of 1765 the Massachusetts economy was badly stressed—a part of a worldwide economic downturn. A drought and the smallpox outbreak the summer before had forced many of the shops and markets to close. Many people were out of work. Then, in May, news reached Boston that Parliament had imposed a Stamp Tax on the colonists: newspapers, legal documents, shipping transfers, any piece of paper used in a business transaction, all had to have a stamp affixed to them.

Even though the Sugar Act clearly stated that it was designed to raise revenue, the reaction to it had come mostly from the merchants and distillers. It had provoked a partial boycott of British made clothing, but to the general public it still resembled a trade tariff. The Stamp Act, however, stirred widespread reaction. This was the blatant imposition of a direct tax and almost everyone would be directly affected. Courts would be shut down and ships would not be able to unload unless the stamps were purchased. Anyone obtaining a liquor license or requesting a marriage license or even just buying a newspaper would have to pay for a stamp. It would take several months for the stamps to arrive in the harbor, but in the meantime the anger in the city grew. Petitions to London seeking repeal of the Sugar Act had proved useless. The colonists needed to find some other way to assert themselves.

John may have known about a meeting that took place at Thomas Chase's distillery on the night of August 13. It was a group of men who called themselves the Loyal Nine, all of whom would be affected by the Stamp Tax: Benjamin Edes, a printer; Henry Bass, a merchant; Joseph Fields, a ship's captain; George Trott, a jeweler; Thomas Crafts, a painter; Stephen Cleverly and John Smith, both braziers; and Thomas Chase and John Avery, both rum distillers. Chase's distillery was near the intersection of Essex and Orange Streets.

Sarah and John would certainly have been aware of the crowd gathered at the end of their street the next morning. It was a Thursday—market day—and the farmer's carts had started rumbling across the neck and up Orange Street even before dawn. When they reached Essex Street, and the lovely cluster of elm trees, some of them stopped to see what was happening. A crude figure marked with the letters A.O., for Andrew Oliver, the Boston merchant who had taken the job of collecting the new Stamp Tax, was hanging from one of the branches of the largest tree. Beside it was a boot with a devil's face sticking out at the top—a pun on the name of the Earl of

Bute who was thought to be one of the masterminds of the tax. It was a jovial enough gathering in the beginning. Some of the farmers allowed a mock stamp to be placed on their goods. The children, out of school, started marching around the tree.[1] Sarah's brother Josiah, then eleven years old, may have been the first in the family to take part in a Boston demonstration against taxation without representation.

By evening the mood had changed. Fifty "gentlemen actors, disguised in Trawsers and Jackets"— the outfits of day laborers—cut down the effigy, put it in a coffin, and set out in a funeral procession through the streets of Boston. A huge crowd followed. At the Town House, where Governor Francis Bernard and his council were meeting upstairs, they gave out three loud huzzas, the old British battle cry. Then they turned down King Street to the end of the wharf where they destroyed the little tax office that had been built to administer the stamps when they arrived from England. Not content with this act of defiance, the mob ran to Andrew Oliver's house where they broke windows and smashed furniture and drank up the wine in his wine cellar.[2] The authorities were powerless. The Sheriff and Lieutenant Governor Hutchinson were pelted with stones when they tried to approach the crowd. When Governor Bernard called for the militia drummers to beat the alarm he was informed that they were all part of the mob.[3]

The next morning Andrew Oliver resigned his appointment and the big elm at Hanover Square was again decorated—this time with lanterns and victory signs. The "Liberty Tree" had become the focal spot for political demonstrations. A few days later the homes of three other government officials became the targets of the same mob violence. They attacked the houses with axes and destroyed almost everything at the grand home of Lieutenant Governor Hutchinson, including the manuscript of Hutchinson's *History of the Massachusetts Bay Colony*—a work on which he had labored for many years. It was by any standard an appalling display of uncontrolled violence.

Or perhaps it had not been totally uncontrolled. Street gangs were a part of Boston life. Fights between the North End and South End gangs were common and sometimes in the night Sarah would have heard the shrill whistle that signaled another ruckus. The annual Pope's Day celebration always culminated in a battle between the two gangs.

These latest mob actions were something more. Accounts of the August 14 demonstration described the participants in the mock funeral procession as "fifty gentleman actors" disguised as day laborers. Even if they themselves were not part of the mob destruction that followed, they had good reason to encourage the gang elements of the city to do so. Publicly, respectable citizens distanced themselves from any knowledge of these events, blaming them on "people of the lower sort." Privately some saw these acts of intimidation as the only way to protect their rights.[4] Governor Bernard repeatedly pressed the Massachusetts House of Representatives for compensation for the citizens whose houses had been vandalized, but the legislators maintained that the town's people could not be held responsible for the actions of "outsiders." Some years later, when the tea was dumped in Boston harbor, the people would insist that they could not be held responsible for the actions of a bunch of "Indians."

There was a growing sense of common purpose. Men with diverse social, business, and political contacts gathered together to discuss their options. In the churches, where membership cut across all social strata, opposition to British policies became a main topic of conversation. Politics had always been fair game for Boston's clergy, and many of them railed against the Stamp Act. One of the most outspoken champions of the patriotic movement was the West Church's Reverend Jonathan Mayhew. Sarah's brother, Samuel, would have recounted his sermons to the rest of the Bradlee clan. Benjamin Edes, one of the Loyal Nine and the printer of the unabashedly patriotic *Boston Gazette*, was also a member of this congregation. At New South, where so many of Sarah's family were members, the congregation included Sam Adams and Thomas Crafts, one of the Loyal Nine. During the Revolutionary War, Sarah's brother David would become a captain in Colonel Crafts' regiment and his son eventually married Crafts' daughter.[5]

It was said that Sam Adams and his "Sons of Liberty" had encouraged the mob actions. Mr. Adams was well known in Boston. He was an outspoken proponent of the rights of the colonists, and he and the "Sons of Liberty" held secret meetings—sometimes in one of the distillery offices near John and Sarah's—to discuss ways of furthering the cause of colonial liberty. Anger at the British was beginning to spread to the other American colonies, and the Sons of Liberty made it their business to coordinate opposition to the Stamp Act with them. New York and Philadelphia were the first to implement a plan to stop importing British goods, and Boston soon followed suit.[6]

Coupled with mob intimidation, non-importation was a powerful weapon for combating British tax laws. But it was an imperfect one. It required the cooperation of many different people and affected them in many different ways. Those who did not abide by the rules might find themselves subject to the taunts of an angry crowd. Certain items were exempt from the boycott. Rich merchants with a healthy inventory would have a stockpile of goods ready for immediate sale when the boycott was lifted. Poorer merchants would have to wait months for new items to arrive. Dockworkers of all kinds would suffer if there were no ships to unload, while local artisans might find their products in high demand as people looked for substitutes for British goods. Sarah's father may have done a brisk business as a weaver during that time.

On November 1, the first day the stamps were scheduled to be issued, the Liberty Tree was again the gathering point for a mass demonstration. More effigies were hung on its branches, and church bells tolled as for a funeral. By afternoon several thousand people gathered and followed the mock funeral procession to the town gallows where the effigies were hanged. A few weeks later Andrew Oliver was "escorted" to the Liberty Tree and again made to renounce his commission as stamp agent to the waiting crowd. There were no outbreaks of violence at either of these demonstrations. The mass gatherings were enough to intimidate the government officials. With no one to distribute the stamps the customs officials reluctantly allowed the port to be opened so that non-prohibited trade could take place.[7] It was apparent that Governor Bernard was losing control.

The boycott of English goods continued and Parliament eventually succumbed to the economic pressure. The Stamp Act was repealed on March 18, 1766, and three months later a ship arrived in port bearing the official news. Church bells rang, cannons fired, fireworks lit up the sky, and the Liberty Tree was festooned with banners. But relations with England had soured. Parliament had made it clear that the repeal of the Stamp Act had been purely an economic decision and had affirmed its right to tax the colonists by passing the Declaratory Act at the same time.

New taxes, in the form of the Townshend Acts, were not long to follow. Direct taxes on British goods were again to be levied, this time on glass, lead, paint, paper and tea. Perhaps, Parliament reasoned, taxes on commodities, because they seemed more like a tariff, would be better tolerated than the stamp tax had been. In any case, customs commissioners were to be sent to Boston to insure the collection of all taxes and tariffs. And, to add insult to injury, the revenue from the tax would be used to pay the salaries of the royal officials, thus depriving the Massachusetts legislature of its only control over them.[8]

Once again the patriots pushed for a boycott of British goods. Periodic gatherings at the Liberty Tree served to remind the merchants of the possibility of harsh reprisals for disregarding the non-importation agreements. Encouraging the public not to buy imported goods from England reinforced the pressure on merchants. People were exhorted to produce and consume locally made goods. It was a policy that made sense economically as well as politically because of the shortage of hard currency. "Save your money and save your country" urged the patriot press.[9]

This time the women of Boston played an essential role. In a society now used to buying readymade cloth from England, spinning became a political statement. Fabrics like the elegant green damask that Sarah had purchased just a few years before were to be eschewed in favor of homespun. The "Daughters of Liberty" staged huge spinning bees and homespun clothing became a badge of honor. The Bradlee women must have done their share.

The new customs commissioners had arrived in October of 1767, well aware that they might become targets of one of Boston's street demonstrations. They were pointedly reminded of this a few days later during the annual Pope's Day revelry, and again the following March when the anniversary of the repeal of the Stamp Act was celebrated by a large gathering at the Liberty Tree. It culminated in a parade past the houses of the governor and some of the customs officials.[10]

In May, with the British Navy ship Romney conveniently lying in Boston Harbor, the customs officials chose the opportunity to assert their authority by seizing the merchant ship Liberty. Its owner, the wealthy shipping merchant John Hancock, had honed his practice of customs evasion to a fine art, and it was said to be Hancock's vast fortune that was funding much of the activity of the Sons of Liberty. Recently arrived in port, and suspected of having its cargo of Madeira wine offloaded in the middle of the night, the Liberty was commandeered by British sailors from the Romney. The crowd around the wharf immediately took matters in hand. A mob of two to three thousand attacked the officials and drove them off, broke windows in some of their homes, and then destroyed the pleasure boat of one of the officials. The boat was dragged to the Liberty Tree where it was condemned in a mock trial and then to the Common where it was burned.[11] In fear of worse, the customs officials fled to the military fort on the island of Castle William.

7

THE OCCUPIED CITY

Boston had gone too far. Responding to the reports of civil unrest, particularly the harassment of government officials, Parliament sent troops to their rebellious colony. Navy ships sailed into the harbor and British regiments disembarked on October 1, 1768. The townspeople could only watch in silent indignation as the soldiers marched into their town—British troops would not be intimidated by a gathering at the Liberty Tree.

Soon there were more than 4,000 soldiers in the city—one fifth of its population. Sarah was likely awakened each morning to the sound of the drilling of the troops, and even the quiet of the Sabbath day was broken by the noise of military parades. Military discipline included the public whippings of soldiers, and one day a deserter was shot on the Common with all the soldiers made to assemble to watch.

Soldiers were everywhere. It must have been galling to be stopped by one of the many sentries now posted around the city. When they weren't on duty they filled the streets, the shops, and the taverns. They moonlighted, taking jobs away from some of the townspeople. They harassed the locals and the locals harassed them. Tensions ran high, for it was hard to know who most resented the quartering of the soldiers, the people of Boston or the soldiers themselves.

Sarah would have had reason to interact with these unruly intruders, for the redcoats arrived just a month after Mary Bradlee was granted a license to "sell strong drink" at her shop. Helping her mother to serve the customers Sarah would have found herself subject to coarse words and drunken brawls between her neighbors and these unwelcome guests. Her willingness in later years to defy British soldiers may have been nurtured in this little shop

Sarah's father had died just a few weeks before the occupation began. Her mother had wasted no time in finding a way to support herself. Less than a month after Samuel's death "Mary Bradley" was approved by the Selectmen for a license to sell strong drink "at her Shop near Mr. Kneelands, South End."[1] A few months later she was paid four dollars from a widows fund, and the following August she was again licensed to sell strong drink, this time as a retailer "at her House in Auchmutys Lane."[2]

The Bradlees took Samuel's body back to Dorchester and buried him in the Old Dorchester Burying Ground. His stone, which still stands, reads "Here lies the Body of Mr. Samuel Bradlee, who died July 7, 1768, aged 62 years. Blessed are the Dead that die in the Lord, they rest from their Labour and their Works Follow them."[3] He lies next to his brother, John.

Eighteen months after Samuel's death the family was again gathered at a graveside, this time to bury Sarah's brother Samuel. He was only thirty-nine years old. They buried him in Boston's Granary Burying Ground. "Here lyes Buried/the Body of/Mr. Saml Bradlee/who Departed this Life/January the 19th 1770/in the 39 year of his Age."[4]

A much larger funeral procession—perhaps the largest ever seen in Boston—took place three days later. Sarah and her family would certainly have been part of it. Eleven-year-old Christopher Seider, a boy from their neighborhood, had been shot by a customs snitch. On his way home from school, Christopher had stopped to watch a crowd that was harassing one of the merchants who was violating the non-importation agreements, and had been killed by a bullet fired into the crowd. The procession, which began at the Liberty Tree, was led by four or five hundred schoolboys walking in pairs—Josiah and Gershom Spear probably among them. Family and friends were clustered behind the coffin, followed by some two thousand mourners, including many "principal gentlemen and a great number of other respectable inhabitants" of the town.[5] Many more spectators looked on. Christopher was buried in his family's yard on Frog Lane—just across the street from the Liberty Tree,[6] and less than a block from the home of Sarah's sister Mary and her husband, William Etheridge.[7]

The tension between the people of Boston and the soldiers was becoming unbearable. On March 3 a terrible ruckus broke out at the ropewalks near John's old Long Lane meeting house. It began as a fight between Mr. Gray, the owner of the ropewalks, and a British soldier, who got the worst of it. He came back with more soldiers, the rope makers got help from the shipyard workers, and the affair escalated into a brawl involving several hundred men welding pipe-staves, marlin spikes, and anything else they could use as a weapon. The soldiers were no match for the burly dock workers and returned to their barracks more resentful than before.[8]

Two days later, on the evening of March 5, 1770, a lone British soldier was standing guard at the Customs House on King Street. A crowd began to taunt him, so he called for help and, as a few soldiers marched down from the Main Guard, people in the crowd began to throw snowballs and, perhaps, rocks. Someone yelled the word "fire"—most likely not one of the soldiers but someone from the crowd—and suddenly five people in the crowd were hit. Three died instantly, two later. The incident became an immediate propaganda tool for the patriots. Within days Paul Revere had produced an engraving labeled "The Bloody Massacre Perpetrated in King Street," which bore little resemblance to the actual event. In fear of more violence the governor removed the troops from Boston, putting as many as possible in Fort William on Castle Island. Boston's citizens would no longer suffer the indignities of living in an occupied city.

By the time of the Boston Massacre Sarah and John had been married for eight years. Living on Essex Street, just a few steps from the Liberty Tree, they had been squarely in the midst of the events of these tumultuous years. Sarah turned thirty years old in 1770. The demonstrations and mob actions that were spawned under the Liberty Tree had undoubtedly shaped her political consciousness, and she must have been more than just a cautious bystander. Sarah's grandniece, who was forty years old when Sarah died, describes her as "a woman fearing nothing, blunt of speech and rather coarse of manners."[9] In an era when women were expected to acquiesce to the thoughts of men, particularly in regard to politics and government, Sarah would brook no nonsense from others. She was bold enough to speak her mind and courageous enough to act upon her convictions.

8

MEDFORD

In 1772 Sarah and John's fifth child, Lydia, was born.[1] In that same year they moved to Medford. The town was famous for its rum, and John went to work in its distilleries. Medford was one of the oldest settlements in Massachusetts. It had begun as the private landholding of a man named Matthew Cradock, who himself never left England. Nestled on the edge of the Mystic River, about five miles out of Boston, the name Medford is perhaps derived from "Meadow ford"—the place in the meadow where one could ford the river. Cradock's men built the first bridge across the river, on the spot where the present bridge still stands. It remained the only bridge across the river until 1787. Thus the only road out of Boston for travelers going north into New England led right through Medford. "It was part of a great thoroughfare, and was second to none in importance to all travelers from the east and north who were going to Boston."[2] The road would become increasingly important when events propelled the area into war.

The Mystic River was central to the livelihood of the town. In a time when transporting goods overland was a tortuous affair, the ebb and flow of the river, twisting its way back to Boston Harbor, allowed for the easy transport of goods to and from one of America's busiest ports. The products of Medford's industries—most importantly Medford rum, and bricks made from the area's abundant clay pits—were loaded onto flat bottom boats, called lighters, and floated downriver on the outgoing tide. The returning tide brought back a vast array of goods recently arrived in Boston Harbor from all over the world. "Medford, by its river, became quite a center of supply to country traders from New Hampshire and Vermont....Traders here could purchase ivory-handled knives, spring-locks, brass-ware, tin, and pewter...groceries...dry goods, Kent linen cotton, Irish stockings, Turkey mohair, red serge, broadcloth, muffs, ribbons, lace, silks, combs, napkins, yellow taffety, threadlace, gloves, etc."[3,4]

The market place was immediately north of the Cradock Bridge. The "great road" from Boston crossed the bridge and then split into a Y, the one arm leading northeast toward Malden, the other northwest toward Woburn. There, where the roads converged, was the center of town, what would come to be known as Medford Square. A few houses and businesses clustered near the square and several taverns along the main roads stood ready to accommodate travelers. The rest of the town consisted of farms and orchards scattered along the main roads and bordered by the low stone walls so typical of the area. Here and there was a substantial brick mansion, but most of the buildings were made of wood.[5] Behind the town, to the north, the wooded hills rose up sharply, making a particularly delightful backdrop in the fall when the trees burst into color. To the east, the river twisted its way toward Charlestown bordered by meadow-like salt marshes.

It is a testament to this pleasing setting that not only Cradock's agents but also John Winthrop, the first governor of the Massachusetts Bay Colony, chose this spot for their personal estates. Cradock's men settled on the north side of the river in what would become the center of Medford. Winthrop chose for himself a huge tract of land, called Ten Hills Farm, which bordered the south side of the river. A wealthy sugar plantation owner from Antigua, Isaac Royall, eventually bought this property. By the time Sarah and John came to Medford the first Isaac Royall had died and the estate was owned by Isaac Royall, Junior. It was his ancestors who many years earlier had shared a bench with Sarah's ancestors in the meeting house in Dorchester. The Royall family still had roots in Dorchester, and when Isaac Royall, Senior died in Medford in 1737, his body had been taken back to Dorchester to be buried in the same cemetery where Sarah's father would later be interred. The Bradlee and Royall families would have known each other for several generations.

The Royall mansion, one of the most celebrated homes in all of Massachusetts, was about a half mile south of the Cradock Bridge. Its manicured lawns sloped down to the river, stately elms lined the drive up to the house, and, in the elegant gardens behind the house, a gazebo built over the ice cellar provided a cooling respite on sultry summer days. "Through the massive gateway and into the paved court to the west door rolled the stately carriages of the Vassals and other noted families of Boston and vicinity, and Colonel Royall returned the visits in the only chariot which was owned for miles on the north side of Boston."[6] This elegant carriage, with its matching geldings and liveried driver, is depicted in a mural in one of the bedrooms. The Royalls were famous for their lavish entertainments. There were several barns on the property, a stable and coach house, and, most unusual for New England, there were slave quarters. Isaac Royall was one of about twenty slaveholders in Medford. Many of the town's more prominent citizens owned one or perhaps two slaves. Colonel Royall owned as many as twenty-seven.

The "great road" ran through the Royall property and it was there, on the east side of the road, just south of the Cradock Bridge that the Fulton family came to live. They must have rented their home from Isaac Royall.[7] The property seems to have included a house (today marked by a plaque at the present site of the police station) and out buildings, bordered to the south by an orchard. It was a busy spot. With the Admiral Vernon Inn as their neighbor to the north and Blanchard's Tavern directly across the road, they would only have had to step out their front door to encounter travelers from all over New England.[8]

Just south of Sarah and John's orchards, where later Main Street would intersect with the Medford turnpike, was Harry Bond's blacksmith shop. It was a weather-beaten building fronted by a big oak tree. "The wide and open door gave a view of the interior. On one side could be seen a massive framework, into which oxen were driven and secured in a sling while being shod."[9] On the other side the forge glowed with red hot iron. Sarah's children must have enjoyed running down the road to watch Harry at his work, and the shop would have been a natural gathering point for grownups, too. Harry, like John, was of Scotch-Irish descent, and the two must have enjoyed trading stories about their heritage.

To go to work John had only to cross the Cradock Bridge to the town center and turn east into Distill House Lane (today's Riverside Avenue). The distillery, owned by Benjamin Hall, had been run by the Hall family since the early years of the century. Seated on the banks of the river, it was ideally located. Molasses could be easily transported up from Boston and the finished rum sent back down, ready for both foreign and domestic sale. The exact site had been chosen because of an abundance of sweet spring water that bubbled up at that spot. It was this water that was said to make Old Medford Rum the best that money could buy.

West of the town square, between the road to Woburn and the river, were the tanneries. These too belonged to the Hall family. Benjamin Hall was one of Medford's most successful businessmen. He was, as Medford historian Helen Wild put it, "a monopolist" before the term was common. Besides making the best rum in the colonies, he also made the barrels in which to store it. He and his brother Ebenezer had a cattle slaughtering business wherein, after they had sold the meat, Ebenezer tanned the hides, and Benjamin made the tallow into candles. These goods, and others coming into Medford from northern towns, could then be loaded onto Hall's lighters and sent down the river to Boston, or they could be sold at the large wholesale barter store that he maintained in Medford.[10]

Across the road (today's High Street) from the tanneries were five houses, all in a row, "all occupied by the Hall family, four of them brothers, and three of the brothers married to three sisters."[11] "The gardens in back of these houses had flights of stone steps leading up the steep slope, laid out in terraces aflame with nasturtiums and bright with marigolds, primroses, phlox and larkspur and with grapes on trellises at the top, which traced golden lacework against the skyline at sunset."[12] The house that belonged to Isaac Hall is still there today.

A little further along the road to Woburn was Pastor Turell's house and the newly-built meeting house. Old Ebenezer, ordained in 1724, was in failing health. Not wanting to dismiss the man who had served their church for fifty years, the congregation invited Reverend David Osgood to become pastor, but continued to pay Turell's salary until his death in 1778. This change allowed for the expression of the divide that was growing between orthodox and liberal believers in many New England churches. Osgood's ordination was opposed by six members of the congregation, and by Turell himself,[13] because the new clergyman asserted the doctrine of "the total corruption of the human heart by nature, previous to renovating grace, as a cardinal point in revealed religion."[14] After clearly expressing their views, the dissenters acquiesced to the wishes of the rest of the congregation and gave their support to the new minister, but the conflicting theologies would continue to be an issue.

Like everyone else, Sarah and John would have attended church each Sunday, but they apparently never signed the covenant or were accepted into communion in the church in Medford. Perhaps they too found it impossible to declare their belief in the "total corruption of the human heart." They still maintained their ties with the New South Church in Boston, and, after the war, at least two of their youngest children were baptized there. Most of Sarah's family still lived in Boston and she and John probably made frequent trips into the city to visit them. With the stagecoach picking up passengers practically at their front door and depositing them in Boston at the Lamb Tavern, not far from the Liberty Tree, it would have been a convenient way to travel.[15] More likely, they either caught a ride on one of Benjamin Hall's lighters, or they walked to Charlestown and took a ferry across to Boston.

9

THE TEA PARTY

Frequently their destination would have been the corner of Tremont and Hollis Streets where Sarah's brother Nathaniel had recently built himself a house. Sarah's grandniece, writing many years later, relates that "In those days Mr. Bradlee on Saturday night had a salt fish supper, at which neighbors, relatives and acquaintances were always present, the guests generally numbering thirty to fifty: politics and the topics of the day were generally discussed."[1] Nathaniel's neighbors would have included John Crane, Joseph Lovering, Tom Bolter, and Samuel Fenno—all housewrights, and all avowed patriots. His friends would have included the men of the neighborhood fire engine company to which he had been appointed in 1768 and again in 1773.[2]

By the fall of 1773 the main topic of conversation at these suppers would have been tea—that most beloved drink of New Englanders. It was a complicated issue. England's economy was inextricably entwined with the British East India Company, a vast, and increasingly corrupt, trading company that had a monopoly on much of British world trade. Its recent investment in huge amounts of Chinese tea had turned out to be a poor decision, and the tea was wasting away in its warehouses.[3] Most of the tea that the colonists were drinking was being smuggled in from Holland. British tea still carried the tax that had been imposed by the Townshend Acts.

Parliament presumed to appease the colonists by devising a plan to allow the British East India Company to ship its tea directly to the colonies, rather than via London. Even with the added tax, the price would undercut the price of smuggled tea. The plan would bolster the British East India Company, raise revenue for England, and allow Parliament to continue to assert its right to impose a direct tax on the colonists. Certainly the small tax would not induce the colonist to give up so desired a commodity as tea, when they would now be able to pay less for it.

Parliament had again misjudged. The patriots would not swallow the plan. Any direct tax, no matter how small, was a violation of their rights, and opened the door to future, more drastic, taxation. Besides this, the British East India Company was allowed to choose the agents who would sell the tea once it was landed. This threatened to set a precedent for monopolies in the sale of other goods. To make matters worse, the revenue from the tea tax was to be used to pay the salaries of the colonial governor and judges. This was a violation of their rights under the Massachusetts Charter and would deprive them of their only control over these officials.[4] And finally, and perhaps most importantly, Boston was feeling great pressure from other colonies not to allow the tea to be landed.

In the eyes of some of the other colonies Boston already had a less than sterling record in its adherence to the non-importation agreements. Throughout the boycott her merchants had continued to purchase some tea from Britain, although in much smaller quantities, while Philadelphia and New York had relied almost entirely on smuggled tea. The patriots in New York, Philadelphia, and Charleston, S.C. had forced the resignations of the tea agents in their colonies, while the agents in Boston, with the backing of Governor Hutchinson, had refused to be pressured. If Boston allowed its tea to be unloaded, it would ruin it for everyone.⁵ In one letter from the Sons of Liberty in Philadelphia, the Bostonians were reminded that "our tea consignees have all resigned, and you need not fear, the tea will not be landed here nor at New York. All that we fear is that you will shrink at Boston. May God give you virtue enough to save the liberties of your country!"⁶

By late November, the Dartmouth, laden with the first shipment of East India Company tea, had arrived at Griffin's Wharf. Two more ships soon followed. A huge town meeting had filled the Old South Meeting House. The people had petitioned Governor Hutchinson to have the ships sent back rather than let them be unloaded and pay the tax, but their petition had been denied. Royal Navy ships were positioned at the mouth of the harbor to prevent the ships from leaving port without having first unloaded the tea, and the law required that a ship's cargo be unloaded within twenty days of its arrival in the harbor. By December 16, the twenty-day period for the unloading of the Dartmouth was about to expire—the next day customs officials would seize the tea and the consignees of the British East India Company would be allowed to sell it. A great crowd again assembled at Old South, where they waited for the Governor's answer to a second petition.

Anticipating that it would not be granted, Nathaniel Bradlee's kitchen had been the scene of furtive activity that afternoon, as Sarah and her sister-in-law Ann worked to create crude Indian disguises for John, and Sarah's brothers, Nathaniel, David, Josiah and Thomas.⁷ This would be Sarah's first clearly defined role in the road to the Revolutionary War. In an account similar to that found in Drake's *Tea Leaves*, Sarah's grandniece Mary Eaton recounts, "I remember what Mrs. Bradlee told me took place in that kitchen.

Nathaniel Bradlee, his brothers, David, Josiah and Thomas met in that same kitchen on the afternoon that the tea was destroyed from the ships in the harbor; their faces were colored and persons disguised by Mrs. Bradlee and a sister of Mr. Nathaniel Bradlee, Mrs. John Fulton of Medford. These four brothers then joined that party that threw the tea overboard and contributed their efforts to one of the events that led to the Revolutionary war."[8] Mary Eaton's letter does not mention John Fulton as one of the participants of the Boston Tea Party, but he is included in both Drake's *Tea Leaves* and Wild's *Medford in the Revolution*. Several of the other housewrights in Nathaniel's neighborhood were also preparing for the tea party, as was Sarah's brother-in-law William Etheridge.[9]

It was early evening when the assembly at Old South finally received word that Governor Hutchinson had again refused to honor their petition. This announcement seemed to be a signal to the waiting "Indians" to set out immediately for Griffin's Wharf. They boarded the ships and dumped 342 chests of tea into the water. "The deed was not that of a lawless mob, but the deliberate and well-considered act of intelligent, as well as determined, men....There was no noise nor confusion. They worked so quietly and systematically that those on shore could distinctly hear the strokes of the hatchets."[10] The crowd that followed them to the wharf, Sarah among them,[11] "looked on in silence during the performance. The night was clear, the moon shone brilliantly, no one was harmed and the town was never more quiet."[12]

On their return to the Bradlee house the two women had a great copper boiler ready with hot water to wash the dye from the men's faces. Nathaniel Bradlee's principles were well known, and a British soldier, hoping to find some proof against him, peered in at the window.

"He found them in bed and to all appearances asleep, they having slipped into bed without removing their "toggery," and feigning sleep."[13] The spy saw the two women seemingly intent on washing clothes at the tub of steaming water. It was their nonchalant behavior that convinced the spy that he had been mistaken in his suspicions and saved the men from capture.

From that day on there was no question but that Sarah was fully committed to the patriot cause. The "tea party" was the pivotal event on the road to the Revolutionary War, the culmination of all the other mass demonstrations that had taken place in Boston since those first two effigies were set swinging on the Liberty Tree on the morning of August 14, 1765. It was a brilliantly thought out and brilliantly executed plan. The "Indians" had prevented the tea from being unloaded in Boston Harbor without causing harm to any other property or person. They had even swept the decks before they left the ships. But it was also a criminal act, and for many—those who, like the Fultons and the Bradlees, were established members of the community—the decision to take part in the destruction of property must have been a weighty one. The names of the participants were well-guarded family secrets for many years.

In his book about the Boston Tea Party, Benjamin Carp says, "You could tell how close a Tea Party man was to the inner circle by how seriously he took his disguise. The eighteen "chiefs" were so thoroughly disguised that they even pretended to speak exclusively in Indian tongue. The men under their command, who had been given some advance notice of the Tea Party, cobbled together the best disguises....At the bottom of the Tea Party hierarchy...[were] the shabbiest disguises or none at all."[14] Sarah must have been privy to the planning of the "tea party", for Drake tells us that she had made preparations for the disguises for John and her brothers a day or two earlier.[15]

The colonists knew the "tea party" would have consequences and Britain retaliated with the Boston Port Bill. It took five months for the news of their fate to reach them. When it did it was worse than they could have imagined. The Boston port was to be closed. Warships would line the mouth of the harbor to insure that all commercial activity would cease. The people would be made to subsist on whatever provisions could be carted in by the narrow neck. A new governor, General Thomas Gage, was being sent, along with more troops to keep order. Massachusetts would now be under military rule, her charter revoked and her government dissolved. The severity of this punishment caused the other American colonies to take notice. Could something like this happen to them? The result was that twelve of the thirteen colonies sent representatives to a Continental Congress meeting in Philadelphia. A common bond was beginning to develop among the colonies.

With the closing of the port, Boston became a bleak, sad town. Many people left, others stayed to protect their homes and businesses, or because they had nowhere else to go. Outside of Boston, Medford would suffer more than most of the other Massachusetts towns, for it ended the lightering business and all the revenue that went with it.[16] The distillery business would be seriously affected.

As tensions increased, the patriot groups began to strengthen their militias and stockpile gunpowder outside of Boston. Militias had always been a part of colonial life, growing out of the need for isolated settlements to protect themselves from Indians. Later they were called upon to fight alongside British troops in the French and

Indian wars. Their leaders were given commissions by the British government, but the militias were never trained in the manner of the British troops.

Gunpowder was in short supply for the colonists. It was apparent to all that the best way for Gage to prevent a rebellion would be to take possession of the colonial munitions. Medford, and other nearby villages, stored their supply of gunpowder in an old grain storage silo a little south of town. The "Powder House" still stands today. Concerned that the British troops would confiscate the powder, Medford acted on August 27 to remove its share to a safer place. The other towns were not so quick. On September 1 General Gage sent British soldiers up the Mystic River. They landed at Ten Hills Farm, marched to the Powder House, and seized 250 casks of gunpowder.

The entire incident, the first real act of aggression against the colonists, took place so near to John and Sarah's house that they must have been aware of it from the moment the ship was sighted on the Mystic River. The following day hundreds of militiamen marched to Cambridge, just across the Charles River from Boston, fearful of what the British soldiers might do next. A plaque on the Powder House marks this event as "the first occasion on which our patriotic fore-fathers met in arms to oppose the tyranny of King George III." To the British, the realization that so many patriots could assemble so quickly must have been unnerving.

It was time for these quiet little Massachusetts towns to make some hard decisions, choices that could put them clearly in conflict with the British government. On November 14, 1774, the people of Medford voted to cease paying their provincial taxes. The taxes were collected and held until they could decide what should be done with them.[17]

. A few weeks earlier, in defiance of General Gage's orders that the colonial government be dissolved, the ninety representatives from throughout Massachusetts had met in Salem and formed the first Provincial Congress. Benjamin Hall, Medford's elected representative, was chosen by the Congress to be one of the Committee of Supplies (a committee to provide ammunition and stores). "His business capacity and his large acquaintance with traders in and out of the province made it possible for him to collect large quantities of goods in his warehouses without arousing suspicion. The commodities in which he dealt were just what the colonies needed in preparing for the impending struggle."[18] Beside the obvious need for military stores, meat and rum were essential troop needs. Thus the warehouses on the Mystic River, where John was working, were soon to become a supply depot for the patriot army. As bookkeeper, John would have kept track of the coming and going of all these supplies.

10

THE WAR BEGINS

In each town the most able men of the militia were organized into an elite group—the Minutemen—ready to be called up at a minute's notice. Benjamin Hall's brother, Captain Isaac Hall, who lived just across the bridge from John and Sarah, commanded the Medford men. As the new year of 1775 began, everyone knew it was only a matter of time before General Gage would again send out troops to search for more of the patriot's munitions and supplies—much of which was now stored in the village of Concord. Medford had sent at least one large consignment to Concord in March.

There was also concern that Gage would try to capture Sam Adams and John Hancock. If caught, they would surely be shipped back to England and found guilty of treason in the English courts. In Boston, some of the Sons of Liberty heard rumors that the British planned to raid Concord on April 19. The road to Concord would take the soldiers through the town of Lexington where Adams and Hancock were staying.

The night before, as soon as they were sure of the British plans, Paul Revere and Will Dawes set out to warn the villages. Revere rode out from Charlestown, but it was only by chance that he ended up riding through Medford. A short way along the road to Lexington he was blocked by British soldiers, posted there by General Gage with the express purpose of thwarting any messengers who might be out to spread the alarm. Revere doubled back, outrunning the soldiers, and took the road through Medford instead. He galloped past

Sarah's house, crossed the bridge, stopped long enough to warn Captain Isaac Hall, and then headed on to Lexington. Within minutes the whole town was roused.

Forewarned of the approaching British soldiers, Adams and Hancock were hidden in the woods outside of Lexington. The little band of about seventy Lexington Minutemen, mustered on the village green, was fired upon by the approaching British soldiers. Eight were killed, nine were wounded. The soldiers continued on to Concord where they did find and destroy some of the hidden supplies, but the villagers managed to keep most of it concealed. Colonial militia and British regulars met at the Concord Bridge, shots were fired, and the British retreated.

Then, as the British started their march back to Boston, minutemen from all the nearby villages, including fifty-nine men from the Medford militia, caught up with them. The British were used to fighting in formation. As they retreated in confusion back to Boston, the minutemen fired at them from behind the cover of trees and fences—the way they had learned to fight against the Indians and the French. In the end the British suffered about 250 killed or wounded and the colonists about 100. Having chased the Redcoats back to Boston, the colonists immediately surrounded the city, intent on keeping General Gage and his army trapped there. The news of what had happened in Lexington and Concord, much of it greatly exaggerated, spread like wildfire throughout the New England colonies. Within two days there were 20,000 men in camps around Boston. One of these camps sprang up in Medford.

Col. John Stark, commander of the New Hampshire militia, is said to have been on his way within ten minutes of hearing the news of the battle.[1] He headed for Medford, established his field office headquarters at the Admiral Vernon Tavern, next door to Sarah and John, and was soon joined by some 1,200 loyal New Hampshire men. The recruiting process took place across the street at Blanchard's Tavern. The mansion so recently abandoned by Isaac Royall became Stark's headquarters, and his wife, Molly, soon joined him there. Stark was a tough old soldier, a veteran of the French and Indian Wars, who years earlier had survived Indian captivity. Both he and his right hand man, Major Andrew McClary, were exceedingly well regarded by their troops. McClary, six feet six inches tall, with a fine athletic build and a booming voice, was perhaps the handsomest man in the colonial army.[2]

Medford had been turned upside down, and Sarah and John were squarely in the middle of it all. Their home was used by some in General Stark's regiment, and from her front door Sarah would have been privy to all the comings and goings of his troops. This was the beginning of the yearlong siege of Boston, the year in which Sarah's mettle would be tested and she would earn her epitaph "Heroine of the Revolution."

In the spring of 1775 a motley array of colonial troops surrounded Boston. Sarah's brothers were among them. Like many other women, Ann Bradlee, whose youngest child had died just a month after the battle at Lexington and Concord, stayed in Boston, determined to protect their home from the British troops.[3] The provincial troops were anything but an army. The men had come at a moment's notice, in response to the fear of an immediate threat, and in the following weeks would feel justified in leaving if they felt so inclined. They were dirty and undisciplined and desperately needed money, arms, supplies and leadership if they were going to have an army capable of holding the British in Boston.

Immediately after Lexington and Concord, Sam Adams and John Hancock departed for the second meeting of the Continental Congress in Philadelphia. But Massachusetts could not wait for Congress to help. By chance, colonial soldiers guarding the Boston neck at Roxbury found out that General Gage planned to break out of Boston for an attack on June 18. The patriots had to take the offensive. With picks and shovels as well as guns three of the regiments near Cambridge sneaked across the Charlestown neck the evening of June 16 and spent the night furiously building a line of protective earthworks on Breed's Hill. They had been sent to fortify the more northerly Bunker Hill, a site that would have been much less threatening to the British in Boston. Somehow Breed's Hill had been chosen instead.[4] The British awoke the next morning to see the colonial troops waiting for them just across the Charles River.

At "9:00 a.m., Major John Brooks, a twenty-three-year-old doctor from Medford, began the three-and-a-half-mile walk [from Charlestown] to Cambridge" to get reinforcements.[5] Early in the day Stark sent several hundred troops to fight in Colonel Wyman's regiment. Readying his troops for battle Stark had been so short of ammunition that he could only give one cupful of powder, fifteen balls and a flint to each of his men. In the afternoon Stark and the rest of his brave New Hampshire troops were called into the fray.[6] They would prove to be a vital addition to the provincial fighting force.

By mid-afternoon the British troops, having been ferried across the Charles River to what they must have assumed would be an easy victory, were being systematically mowed down as they came within range. It turned out to be a costly, bloody battle and in the end nearly half the British soldiers were either killed or injured. The people of Boston, crowded together on every possible vantage point, watched the carnage in fascinated horror.

In Medford, where people had earlier been awakened by the sound of cannon fire, one could only wait in fear for news of the fate of their troops. After Stark's men had left Medford, Sarah and others hastily readied a makeshift hospital in the field across the street from her house. As the afternoon wore on the anxiety to know what was happening became unbearable. Did Sarah know that her youngest brother Josiah was among those on Bunker Hill that day?[7] Or did she, like so many townspeople, spend the day in the agony of not knowing which units had been sent to battle, and which loved ones might perish that day? She and her family would have been among those "huddled in little groups on Pasture Hill, or on the marshes, hearing the boom of cannon, seeing the smoke of burning Charlestown, but, on account of the position of Bunker and Breed's hills, seeing only a part of the actual battle."[8]

It was lack of ammunition that finally forced the patriots to retreat. Colonel Prescott's purported admonition, "Don't fire until you see the whites of their eyes," was a reminder that they must let none of their precious ammunition be wasted. Stark had instructed his men not to shoot until they could see the soldiers' half-gaiters—coverings worn on their lower leg.[9]

By late afternoon news of the battle began to filter back to the townspeople, some of it reported by Major McClary who had returned briefly to gather dressings for his wounded men. Toward evening they began to bring the dead and the wounded back to Medford, and lay them out on the ground of the crude field hospital. Sarah would never forget this night. Its horrors would forever be etched in her mind's eye.

Among the dead was Major McClary. That beautiful man whom they had armed with bandages for his wounded men just a few short hours before was suddenly no more. Returning to the front he had been hit by a cannon ball fired from one of the British ships wreaking havoc at the Charlestown Neck.[10] His riderless horse had found its own way back to Medford.[11] Sarah and John's neighbor, Harry Bond, was another of those killed that day.[12] But Sarah did not allow herself the luxury of grieving, and under the direction of Medford's Dr. Simon Tufts[13] she set about her task of easing the suffering of those who were still living. Years later when one of the soldiers came to thank her for having dug a bullet out of his torn cheek she confessed that she hardly remembered having done it. It had been but one small wound in a night filled with so many ghastly wounds.[14]

In spite of the fact that the patriots had finally retreated, they had delivered a devastating, and totally unexpected, blow to the British army. Over 1,000 of the 2,200 British soldiers engaged in the fight had been killed or wounded. The patriots had suffered 115 dead and 305 wounded.[15] There was now no doubt that they were at war with England. George Washington was appointed by the Continental Congress to lead the patriot troops and was immediately sent to Cambridge where he took command on July 3. The colonial forces became the Continental Army. Washington was appalled at the condition of his "army," and yet they had proved themselves at Bunker Hill to be fiercely determined fighters. Their job now was to prevent the British from getting out of Boston and they worked continuously to build huge defense works.

The summer of 1775 was dreadful. Many people had been left homeless by the burning of Charlestown and soon thereafter General Gage forced many of the patriots out of Boston. Medford was one of the first places of refuge for these people. Among those who came from Boston were three who were probably related to John—Captain Robert Wier and John Fulton were probably his cousins, and Robert Fulton was either a cousin or a brother.[16]

People suspected that Gage was purposely sending people out of Boston who were infected with smallpox. In hopes of protecting themselves from this dreaded disease they had a smokehouse on the main road just a little south of the Royall House. Everyone entering the town had to stop and be smoked. The danger, however, turned out to be dysentery. Besides the influx of refugees there were about 1,000 troops stationed in or near the little town. There wasn't nearly enough food or housing. Sanitary conditions were deplorable, and many people got sick. Fifty-six of the Medford townspeople died that year, and twenty-three of them were children.[17] Five-year-old Mary Fulton was one of those children. Despite all their efforts, in the end the family was helpless to do anything but try to comfort her as she passed away. Mary died on October 10, and her grieving family laid her to rest in the Burying Ground near the town square. Her grave marker is still there today.

The Tilden family papers on file at the DAR say that little Frances Burns, then fifteen months old, was baptized at Medford's First Parish three days after her sister's death. Perhaps her parents had planned to wait until they could go back into Boston to baptize her at the New South Church—as they did with at least two of their later children, Samuel and Lucretia. With death so ever-present it must have seemed unthinkable to wait.[18]

That winter was exceptionally cold. The Committee of Supplies ordered 1,300 coats to be made for the patriot soldiers, and Medford women made sixty of them.[19] The soldiers in both armies were freezing. Wood was so scarce that British soldiers frequently sneaked across the Mystic River to the woodlots around Medford in search of fuel.

"One day a load of wood intended for the troops at Cambridge was expected to come through town, and one of these bands of (British) soldiers was there before it. Sarah, knowing that the wood would be lost unless something was done, and hoping that private property would be respected, sent her husband to meet the team, buy the load, and bring it home. He carried out the first part of the programme, but on the way to the house he met the soldiers, who seized the wood."[20]

Sarah was not about to surrender that precious wood without a fight. In those last few years in Boston she had been well schooled in thumbing her nose at British soldiers. As soon as John told her what had happened she flung on a shawl and ran out of the house in pursuit of the thieves. Overtaking them, she reached up, grabbed one of the oxen by the horn and forced it to turn around. The soldiers, astonished at her audacity, threatened to shoot her. Her response was simply to square her small shoulders and challenge them to "shoot away!" Without a backward glance she led the oxen down the road and into her own yard. The soldiers were left looking after this bold little woman with begrudging admiration.[21] Within a few weeks she would prove just how bold she really was.

John Brooks, later elected governor of Massachusetts, was to become one of Medford's most noted citizens. Born in Medford, he was a physician in the nearby town of Reading when the Revolution began. He led a company of minutemen from that town at the Battle of Lexington and Concord, and was made a major in the Continental Army after Washington arrived to take command. During the war he rose to the rank of lieutenant-colonel and became a friend of General Washington.[22] In 1776, near the end of the siege of Boston, Major Brook's regiment took part in Washington's secret preparations to force the British out of Boston by fortifying Dorchester Heights.

"Major Brooks...was given dispatches by General Washington which must be delivered inside the enemy's lines. Late one night he came to John Fulton, knowing his patriotism and his intimate knowledge of Boston, and asked him to undertake the trust. He was not able to go," but Sarah, who knew the streets of Boston just as well as John did, volunteered to go in his place.[23] Sarah's grandniece Mary Eaton says that Sarah herself recounted to her both this story and the story of the wood, and that Sarah undertook to deliver Washington's messages because John "did not dare to take them."

Sarah did not hesitate. She grabbed up her sewing basket, snipped away a few threads in the hem of her skirt, and slipped the papers into the opening. Then it took just a few quick stitches to close the slit and insure that those precious communications were well hidden.[24] Leaving John and the children to spend a worrisome night, she wrapped herself in her warmest cloak and set out into the raw night air down the road to Charlestown. Sarah had walked that road countless times, but never alone in the middle of the night, never with the fearful knowledge that there were lives, including her own, depending upon her. Soon she had gone past the huge stone posts that marked the stately carriage entrance to Isaac Royall's mansion. It was no longer the elegant carriages of the Royall family and their privileged guests who used that gracious entryway. Isaac Royall had gone to Boston the day of the Battle of Lexington and Concord and never returned. The soldiers' rough boots and the heavy hooves of their horses had since trampled the grounds of what had become Colonel John Stark's military headquarters.

Between tiny Two-Penny Brook and Winter Brook were mostly open fields and orchards, and beyond was the military encampment on Winter Hill that General Stark's soldiers had built. After the Battle of Bunker Hill they had been so sure that the British would attack that those poor exhausted men had started work on it the next night. The attack had never come and the patriots had managed to keep the British holed up in Boston for nearly a year.

By the time Sarah reached the intersection with the road to Cambridge she was almost to the Charlestown neck. Then began the most perilous part of her journey. She had to cross the narrow bit of land that connected the mainland with British occupied Charlestown. It was a barren stretch of land—at high tide only about thirty feet across at the narrowest point.[25] Were there no sentries posted there? Would she somehow manage to sneak past them undetected? Could she perhaps contrive to beguile them with a coy story?

Beyond the neck, she had about a mile to go before she would reach the Charlestown beach. Bunker Hill, fortified by the British, rose off to her left and below it was Breed's Hill, where the battle had actually been fought. On her right she skirted along the charred ruins of the village of Charlestown. In the dark she could have only seen the ghostly shape of a fireplace or chimney jutting up here and there. The British had torched the town during the Battle of Bunker Hill. Anything that hadn't burned then had been hauled away during the winter to serve as firewood.

Reaching the water's edge she found an abandoned boat and stepped in, taking great care not to wet the hem of her skirt. The bitter ocean air cut through her, and her hands ached with cold. Memories of loved ones drowned years before in Boston's treacherous waters must have played on her mind as she steeled herself to carry out her trusted mission. She grasped the oars of the little boat, prayed that she would not be spotted, and rowed the half-mile across the Charles River to Boston's north end. It would have taken all her strength to do this. The Charles River was a tidal river. Paul Revere had had two men to row him across at this same spot on the night of April 18.

Once inside Boston, she had to avoid the British patrols. Willing away the thoughts of what might happen to her if her mission were to be discovered, she wended her way through the familiar streets. Even in the dark she would have seen the deplorable conditions that people here were enduring. Finding her destination, she tapped lightly at the door and quickly extracted Washington's papers from their hiding place. A few whispered words, and then the door was quietly shut. Alone again in the dark, she must have longed to run to see those of her family who had remained in Boston—they were now just a few short blocks away. But she dared not risk it. Instead she turned back the way she had come and retraced her steps to her own dear home.[26]

What was the message in the papers so carefully concealed in Sarah's skirt? It must have been nearly the beginning of March when she made her perilous journey, because before then the Charles River was frozen over and it would have been impossible for her to have rowed across.[27] It may be that she was sent to warn the patriots inside Boston of Washington's impending attack from Dorchester Heights. Washington had tried for months to devise a plan to force the British out of Boston, and had waited impatiently for Knox's men to arrive with the cannon they had dragged from Fort Ticonderoga. When they finally appeared he prepared the assault from Dorchester Heights as quickly as he could. The patriots inside Boston needed to be alerted, especially those in Boston's South End, where Sarah would have known every nook and cranny. Major Brooks, who sent her, took part in fortifying the Heights of Dorchester[28] and so would have been privy to its planning.

Whatever the message, it must have been one of great importance for Brooks to allow Sarah Fulton to risk her life to deliver it. Of all her acts of courage and patriotism, this was Sarah's shining moment. It was a deed that would be remembered for the rest of her life—and beyond—and honored by some of the most important people in our nation's history.

The fortification of Dorchester Heights forced the British out of Boston. Troops and loyalist civilians scrambled to get themselves and a few possessions onto ships and on March 17 they evacuated Boston.[29] Patriots from the nearby villages wasted no time reuniting with those loved ones who had been trapped in Boston. On March 22 "a concourse of people from the country" crowded into Boston, "full of friendly solicitude...and fond embraces of those who have been long separated."[30] Sarah and John must have been among them, happily embracing the family and friends they had worried over during that long year, sadly surveying the wreckage of their beloved Boston. The Liberty Tree was only a raw stump.

Throughout the colonies the talk turned to independence. The next few months would see the Congress in Philadelphia in hot debate over the issue of declaring a formal break from England. By putting their names on such a document the signers would risk being hanged for treason.

At a town meeting in Medford in June the people unanimously voted that if the "Honorable Continental Congress, for the safety of the United Colonies, declare them independent of the Kingdom of Great Britain, the inhabitants of this town will solemnly engage with their lives and fortunes to support the measure."[31] In the next several years many of them would do just that.

Congress finally produced the Declaration of American Independence on July 4, 1776. Two weeks later, Colonel Thomas Crafts, John and Sarah's friend from New South, stepped out on the balcony of the Boston State House and read the document to the waiting crowd.

11

THE WAR MOVES ON

With the British out of Boston, Washington and his army moved on to what would become eight long years of war. Boston and its surrounding towns, always fearful that the British would return, did what they could to support the army. Sarah and her oldest daughters were surely among those women who "carded, spun, knit and sewed the much needed clothing for the army."[1]

Medford, like the rest of Massachusetts, sent troops to Washington's army. Muster rolls are incomplete and men from one town were often recruited by other towns, but Helen Wild, in *Medford in the Revolution*, says that there were over 200 men who served for Medford— about a quarter of the population. Congress imposed repeated drafts and quotas, and, like every other community, Medford struggled to fill hers, either by enlistments or by paying bounty.

In July of 1776 they had particular difficulty finding men willing to enlist for an expedition to Canada —the memory of the terrible defeats at Quebec and Montreal the year before was still too fresh. Eventually three of the Hall brothers advanced the town L240 for bounty money. Smaller amounts were added by many of Medford's other citizens, including John Fulton who loaned money for bounty for this expedition and again in September for troops needed in New York.[2]

There is no record that John Fulton ever served in the army, but he may have been an important link in keeping the army supplied. Throughout the war Benjamin Hall's warehouses served as a supply depot for the patriot army. "Powder in large quantities was collected there and 'boated' to Boston when needed. In 1779 and 1780 sixteen tons of cannon balls were stored by Mr. Hall for eighteen months. Large quantities of beef were packed by him in barrels made on the premises, and shipped in his lighters, for the use of the army.[3] Rum was essential to maintaining the army, and Benjamin Hall's distillery was the source of much of this rum. One observer calculated that the rebel soldiers "were consuming a bottle per day per man."[4]

As the armies moved away from Massachusetts, those left at home were to endure years of interminable anxiety. They feared for their soldiers gone off to fight. They feared for themselves should the British return to New England. Their darkest fear was that the war would be lost and they would forever be colonial subjects of a British government only too ready to punish them for their temerity.

Pastor Osgood, reflecting on the war a decade later, spoke of it as a time "when hope was deferred and the heart sickened with pain and anguish, [when the years] seemed without end, [and] a burden lay upon my spirits by day and by night almost too heavy for frail mortal to sustain . . . Thus, daily lamenting and praying against the miseries of the war, I passed through that most gloomy portion of my past life."[5]

Stories trickled back of defeat and retreat for the patriot army, but finally word reached them of Washington's Christmas Day capture of the Hessian troops at Trenton. Burgoyne's surrender at Saratoga on October 17, 1777 brought a real glimmer of hope to their cause. It also brought English troops from the Saratoga battle to Medford as captives. Hessian soldiers were quartered at Winter Hill, and officers at Porter's Tavern in the market place. For the most part they were treated well.⁶ John Brooks, who had become a lieutenant-colonel in the Eighth Massachusetts Regiment, had played an important part in the capture of Burgoyne and his army.⁷ It would be the summer of the following year before anyone there knew that reports of that Saratoga victory had been instrumental in persuading the French to agree to support the patriots against the British. The alliance would prove to be invaluable.

Brooks went on to suffer through the winter of 1777-78 with the troops at Valley Forge, writing back to a friend of his distress at seeing "our poor brave fellows living in tents, bare-footed, bare-legged, bare-breeched... in snow, in rain, on marches, in camp and on duty, without being able to supply their wants."⁸

There were victories and defeats, but the never-ending uncertainty dragged on and on, and the grim news of the British capture of Charleston on May 12, 1780 brought a new wave of despair. Osgood recalled that "after the loss of Charleston, the defeat of General Gates at Camden, and the success of the enemy in over-running the southern states our affairs seemed to be tottering on the brink of ruin. The dejection of the public was at no time greater than towards the close of that year."⁹

Finally, stories of patriot victories in the southern colonies began to filter back. Sarah must have awoken each morning barely daring to hope that the good news would continue. Then, at last, when reports reached them of the defeat of Cornwallis and his surrender of 8,000 troops at Yorktown on October 19, 1781, the people of Medford could not contain their joy. Hauling a barrel of tar onto Pasture Hill they coated wood and rags with the black goo and "immediately celebrated with a huge bonfire."¹⁰ It was not quite the end of the war, but England had lost the will to continue the interminable battles so far from home and before long would relinquish its hold on New York City and Charleston.

The Treaty of Paris was signed in September of 1783. December 11 was declared a national day of thanksgiving and on that day preaching his sermon on *The Goodness of God in Supporting the People* Osgood exulted "Blessed be God! These scenes of misery and distress are now happily closed. Our work is done. The most complete and glorious revolution the world ever beheld, is accomplished."[11] The war that had consumed them all for the past eight years was over, and they were citizens of an independent nation.

Next the question was could they survive as such? The Congress of the United States—the single governing body created by the Articles of Confederation—was virtually powerless. It could not tax or regulate commerce. Those who had been paid in continental currency found it nearly worthless. Many had given most of what they had to support the war. "In 1784 Mr. Hall said, 'When the war began I would not have exchanged property with any man in the country, but now I am worth nothing.'"[12] He and his brothers had lost large sums from furnishing the government with rum and other medical and military supplies and receiving payment in a constantly depreciating currency.[13]

New England suffered more than did the southern states from the loss of trade with Britain and the West Indies. Shipbuilding and the exporting of lumber, whale oil, salted fish and Medford rum were all adversely affected until new trade routes could be established.[14]

12

THE FARM ON THE ROAD TO STONEHAM

In spite of the economic turmoil of these years, Sarah and John were able to buy a house and property on the outskirts of Medford—the only home they ever owned. On July 20, 1782 they purchased, for the sum of L99, property from the estate of one Jane Forkner. The executors of the deed were Simon Tufts Jr. of Medford (d. 1786) and Robert Wyer, Distiller, of Boston, probably related to John.[1] It was on the north side of Medford, not far from Pine Hill, on the old road to Stoneham that rose steeply up through the Charlestown wood lots. Most of the trees there had been cut down for firewood during the terrible winter of the siege of Boston, but new growth had already begun and within time it would again become a densely wooded area.[2]

John and Sarah did not immediately move to their new property, but stayed in the house near the Cradock Bridge for another three years. By then the last of their ten children had been born. In the winter following the siege they had had another child, a daughter, born February 5, 1777.[3] In the manner of the time, they named her Mary, after the other dear little Mary whose death they still mourned. There seems to be no record of her baptism. Perhaps there were omissions in the church records during those tumultuous years. Samuel Bradlee, born March 3, 1779, and Lucretia Butler, born January 10, 1782, were both taken back to Boston to be baptized at New South.[4] Their last child, Elizabeth Scott, was born June 5, 1784, a year after the end of the war.[5]

In the fall of 1784, Lafayette—much revered by the people of America—returned to the newly independent country to visit his beloved George Washington. He toured several cities and was made an honorary citizen in three states, including Massachusetts. It was during this visit that Sarah first met the French hero. Sarah's grandniece, Mary Eaton, relates that Sarah's brother David "was quite wealthy for those days and lived on Brattle Square. On Lafayette's first visit he became well acquainted with David and visited him at his house. A day or two before Lafayette returned to France he persuaded David Bradlee to accompany him, but before he should be able to go he (Mr. Bradlee) must visit his sister, Mrs. John Fulton, who lived in Medford, in rather humble circumstances. So Lafayette [who must have been intrigued by the opportunity to meet this remarkable woman] accompanied him to Medford and was introduced to Mrs. Fulton."[6] It is possible that David, a captain in the Revolutionary Army, would have known Lafayette during the war. They also shared the bond of membership in the Masonic brotherhood.[7] Then a wealthy wine merchant, David's business would have necessitated trips to France and he would have welcomed an opportunity to sail with Lafayette.

In 1785 John and Sarah's oldest daughter, Sarah Lloyd, married Nathan Wait. She may well have worn the same beautiful green damask dress that her mother had worn for her own wedding twenty-three years earlier. The dress shows the marks of repeated alterations, reflecting the changes in fashion that took place over the years. Nathan was a blacksmith. Two years before his marriage he had opened a blacksmith shop on the road to Charlestown, just below the Cradock Bridge and just above the Fulton home. With the taverns and inns nearby and the market square across the bridge, it was a prime location.[8]

Sarah and John most likely moved to the farm at this time and Nathan and Sarah Lloyd took up residence in the old house, so convenient to Nathan's shop. Nathan and Sarah Lloyd would live in this house for the rest of their lives. At the time of their marriage it was still part of the old Royall estate, now held as confiscated property. In 1808 Nathan purchased the house and surrounding land from a syndicate that had bought the property some years earlier.[9] Two of their children would later live on the same street. Nathan William Wait, also a blacksmith, married Susan Smith and built a house a little north of his parents. Eliza Butler Wait married Jonathan Perkins, who built his house a little to the south.[10]

For John and Sarah their new home in the woods must have literally been a breath of fresh air. Gone were the heavy odors of salt water, fish, tar and molasses, gone were the noise and commotion of living directly on Medford's main thoroughfare. Instead the rooster's crow would wake them in the morning and the crickets' chirps lull them to sleep at night. A short hike up Pine Hill would reward them with a view of all of Medford, and, on a clear day, one might see all the way to the ocean.[11]

The farm consisted of about fifteen acres with an orchard and garden near the house and more orchards near the barn. Low walls—stones so carefully piled that no mortar was needed—bordered the road leading to the house. It was a simple wooden house, two stories high, with a small addition, presumably the kitchen, on one side. Their doorstep was a large, flat-topped granite rock. There is a drawing of the house, done many years later, displayed in the Sarah Bradlee Fulton Room at the Royall House. Its frame is made from a piece of a shutter that once covered a window of Nathaniel Bradlee's house in Boston.[12]

13

THE NEW COUNTRY

As the new nation struggled to establish its footing in the world, the increasing awareness of the defects of the national government under the Articles of Confederation finally resulted in the calling of a Constitutional Convention in Philadelphia in 1787. Behind closed doors the delegates set out not to amend the existing Articles of Confederation but to create a completely new document. It took almost four months for the new constitution to be completed. It would not be voted on by the state legislatures, but by a special "Convention of Delegates chosen in each State by the People thereof."[1]

Medford, like the other towns in Massachusetts, called a town meeting to vote for delegates to the convention. The Constitution of the Commonwealth of Massachusetts gave the vote to men over twenty-one years of age, who had lived in their town more than a year, and who owned property worth more than L60.[2] Thus John, who now owned property worth L99, was entitled to vote. Sarah, of course, was not. Medford's own John Brooks, a "zealous advocate" of the proposed document, was one of those chosen to be a delegate to the convention.[3]

When the Massachusetts State Convention began its deliberations in January 1788, five other states had already ratified the constitution with little or no opposition. The approval of at least nine states was required. "The Massachusetts ratifying convention was the first to meet in a state where there was significant opposition to the Constitution." Although the commercial interests of the people of Boston and its environs led them to favor a strong federal government, there were many people, particularly in the rural areas who feared a loss of their newly won freedoms. "If Massachusetts refused to ratify, other states...would probably follow her example."[4] Interest ran high. The Constitution's future might well be decided in Massachusetts.[5]

The State House was not large enough to accommodate the 364 convention delegates plus the many citizens of Boston who came daily to hear the debate, so the convention accepted an invitation from Pastor Jeremy Belknap to meet in his church—John Fulton's old family church on Long Lane. Besides seating the delegates on the floor, the galleries could hold 600 to 800 people. "By January 20, spectators had to arrive an hour early in order to get a seat." By the end of the convention people had jammed themselves into every available nook and cranny, because no one "could say for certain how the final vote would go."[6] Some of Sarah's Boston relatives must have been among the spectators, and perhaps Sarah and John were there too.

On February 7, 1788, the Massachusetts State Convention ratified the new constitution by a margin of only nineteen of the 355 votes, and this only after the Federalists had agreed to recommend that a bill of rights be added to the document. The people of Boston were jubilant. Soon bells all over Boston began to ring, and the "people poured into the streets, shouting 'huzza' and celebrating what was for them a glorious victory."[7] Old Long Lane was renamed Federal Street in honor of this historic event and John's old church became known as the Federal Street Church. How much had changed since the "Presbyterian Strangers" had worshiped in that old barn only sixty years earlier. By the end of summer the requisite number of states had ratified the constitution, and on April 30, 1789 George Washington was inaugurated the first president of the United States of America.

In the fall of that year, President Washington toured the New England states for a month, visiting some sixty towns. Wherever he went he was greeted with great celebrations. Boston was no exception. On October 29 he visited Medford.[8] The day dawned crisp and clear. It was a day of great anticipation in the Fulton household. General Brooks had informed them that George Washington would be passing through town that day and that the President intended to stop to pay his respects to Sarah. The house was scrubbed, the family dressed in their best. Did Sarah perhaps wear the pale green damask dress that is now displayed at the Royall House?

Washington and his small entourage had left Boston on horseback early that morning, stopped in Cambridge and then arrived at General Brooks' house just west of the meeting house for a late breakfast—one that included Indian corn cakes, a favorite of the President. It was the last time General Brooks would ever see his friend. Next door the children had lined up in front of the town school, each student holding his quill pen. Others of the town were dressed in their best and standing on the street hoping to catch a glimpse of their hero.[9]

The President and his little group left the Brooks' house, rode through Medford Square, and turned up the road to Stoneham. The Fulton family, hearing the sound of the approaching horses, knew that their illustrious guest had arrived. A moment later the imposing figure of His Excellency, the President of the United States, was standing in Sarah's doorway. He was the closest thing to royalty her new country would ever know. He removed his hat and bowed to her.

She presented her family to him and offered him their best chair—a Windsor armchair with a high, birdcage style back.[10] The descendants of then ten-year-old Samuel would become the caretakers of this precious piece of furniture. Sarah's new silver punch bowl was filled with John's special punch, made with his prized Old Medford Rum, and Sarah used the little silver-handled ladle to serve their honored guest the first cup of the steaming brew.[11] These too would become cherished family heirlooms. Undoubtedly talk turned to Sarah's meeting with Lafayette, and the hopes for a good outcome for France in its quest for a democratic government.

And then the children would have listened in awe as the most revered man in their new nation expressed his gratitude to their mother for her many selfless acts of patriotism—above all for her willingness to risk her life to deliver his dispatches.[12] All too soon it was time for their honored guest to leave. He bowed to Sarah again, mounted his horse, and rode off to continue his progress across their new country. Sarah was left to bask in the glow of this unforgettable day—a day that would be engraved in her memory for the rest of her life.

That George Washington, in the midst of all the adulation of his tour, took the time to travel to Stoneham to visit Sarah in her home, testifies to the importance of her acts of bravery. After all the years of the war, after all the struggles to form a government for this new country, her courage was still remembered.

It seems that the younger Fulton children made a good impression on their honored guest that day. Washington must have noted how politely and quietly they stood in the background while the grownups carried on their conversation, because within a few hours he had returned with some children-sized chairs. After his visit Washington's horse had thrown a shoe and while he was waiting to have his horse shod he had seen the chairs in a nearby shop and bought them for the Fulton children. Two of these chairs are now in the Royall House in Medford.[13]

How peaceful their quiet country home must have seemed. Sarah and John had spent all their married life in the midst of political strife and the struggles of war. At last they could take great pride in the emerging democracy of their new country and its newly elected government. They had nurtured their children through all those difficult years, and finally the oldest were establishing their own homes. In January of 1789 their oldest son, John Andrews, married Mehitable Owen in New London, Connecticut. He would live in New London for the rest of his life. Another wedding marked the end of that year. Lydia was married to John Bannister on December 31 in King's Chapel in Boston by the Reverend James Freeman—the first Unitarian minister to be labeled as such in the United States. His friend, John Kirkland, later the president of Harvard, was to become minister at New South in 1794.

It may have been about this time that Sarah and John acquired a set of Chinese porcelain dinnerware. There is one small plate that, like the dress, has been passed down from mother to daughter through the generations. It dates from around the turn of the century,[14] a period during which Medford was heavily involved in trade with China.

Sadly, their joys were quickly overshadowed. John Fulton died on February 9, 1790. He had had little time to enjoy his new home or his new country. Pastor Osgood noted in his diary that he attended the funeral. It was a cloudy day, with a light snow. John died of "complications puking."[15] Presumably his death was unexpected and he was still working at the distillery when he died. A receipt for rum and molasses found in his desk many years later is dated February 3d, 1790, just the week before he died.[16] John's health was certainly questionable. He was about forty years old when the Revolutionary War began, and although yet young enough to do so, he apparently never served in the militia or in the army. On the night that Brooks came to their house with Washington's dispatch one source says that John was too ill to go.

His youngest daughter, Elizabeth Scott, stitched a mourning sampler for her father. It is now displayed at the Medford Historical Society.

> *He is gone and his family in tears*
> *How loved how valued once avals the(e) not*
> *To whom related or by whom besot*
> *A heap of dust alone remains of the(e)*
> *Tis all thou art and all the proud shall be*

Sarah, then forty-nine years old, was left a widow to manage the secluded farm on the road to Stoneham. Sarah Lloyd, John Andrews, and Lydia were married and living in their own homes, and gradually her other children married and moved away, except for Ann and Elizabeth, who remained on the farm with Sarah and continued to live there after her death.[17]

Two years after John's death Sarah took up caring for one of the elderly women of the town. For many years the town had paid Rebecca Peirce to sweep the meeting house. Her mother had had the job before her and Rebecca had taken over when her mother could no longer do it. At age seventy-three, Rebecca could not care for herself, and others in the community had been caring for her for the last few years. On May 5, 1791 the selectmen approved a payment of L3.12 for Sarah's expenses in "boarding and nursing Rebecca Peirce." Over the next six years she received regular reimbursements from the town for Rebecca's care. Others in the community made shoes and shifts for Rebecca and after she died, in October of 1797, Sarah received additional recompense for damage to her bed.[18]

Medford, like other New England towns, had long had a practice of "warning out of town" newcomers who they feared would become a financial burden, but the town regularly made provisions for established members of the community who fell on hard times. The selectmen's records routinely contain entries for such care. Nathan Wait is repeatedly paid for caring for one Elizabeth Reed. From September 1806 to July 1813 Sarah again received regular reimbursements from the selectmen. The records for this period are much less detailed, but it appears that Sarah was again caring for one of Medford's needy citizens—this time a woman named Grace Hadley.[19]

We know little else about Sarah's life during these years after John's death, except for a precious bit of information found in two depositions given by Ann and Elizabeth and preserved in the Revolutionary War pension records. The words of her daughters, written little more than a year after Sarah's death, are the closest we come to direct communication with Sarah herself.

In June of 1837 Ann and Elizabeth were called upon to verify the identity of one Polly Johnson (Johnston), a widow of a Revolutionary War soldier, who was applying for a pension. Ann relates that when the Fulton family lived on the road to Stoneham, "Henry Johnson lived with his wife and family in a small house about half a mile from us toward said Town of Stoneham. He, Johnson, was well known to me before that time, having worked with my father in the Distilhouse, while my father lived in the village, but after we removed to the farm, he was our nearest neighbor in that direction, and I saw him much oftener.... After my father's decease said Johnson was frequently called upon to work and perform small jobs and errands for my mother and the family, in which was he was very clever and attentive, though he was often, especially when affected by liquor, very abusive to his wife and children, who were obliged frequently to flee to the neighbors for protection, his wife used often to have recourse to us, on such occasions with some of her young children....After his death in 1801 she had his house removed onto a small piece of land given to her for this purpose by my mother Sarah Fulton and has ever since resided in it and still does so. It stands not twenty rods from the house in which I now reside and in which my father and mother resided until their deceases."[20]

    In the words on these scant two pages we are able to catch a glimpse of Sarah. We see her to be a strong woman, capable of holding her own against a drunken, angry man, and a compassionate woman, making it possible for a widow and her children to keep their home.

    The eighteenth century came to a close with the death of George Washington. He died on December 14, 1799, and the country mourned its loss. Medford held its official day of mourning on January 13, 1800. The men and boys of the town went in procession to the meeting house where the women were already gathered. John Brooks, friend and fellow soldier to Washington, gave the eulogy. The bell tolled until sunset.[21] A host of bittersweet memories must have played through Sarah's mind that day.

14

MEDFORD IN THE NEW CENTURY

The last decade of the century had been filled with political turmoil as the competing factions of Federalists and Anti-federalist Republicans vied to shape the fledgling government to their vision of what the new country should become. Medford, aligned with the commercial and shipping interests of Boston, was firmly in the Federalist's camp. Pastor Osgood spoke out vociferously against the Republican factions and the policies that led to the War of 1812.

The new century brought new prosperity to Medford. Already famous for its rum, the town was to become famous for shipbuilding. It must have taken a lot of Medford rum to build those Medford ships.

More than 500 ships would be built in Medford. By 1844, at the height of the industry, there were ten shipyards within a distance of one mile, "one quarter of the shipbuilders in the Commonwealth were employed in this town, and built nearly one-quarter of the ships constructed in the State, one-third of the tonnage, and one-half the value of the whole."[1] The whole town would make it a holiday to watch the launching of one of these ships.

The Middlesex Canal was built during this same period. It was one of the first of the many barge canals built in the northeastern United States to facilitate the transfer of goods at a time when roads were still so poor that overland transportation was a tedious affair and railroads were still a thing of the future. The Medford shipyards relied heavily on the canal for the delivery of its New Hampshire lumber supplies. Once completed, the canal made a picturesque addition to Medford life. There were passenger-packets that provided leisurely travel. "Seated under a capacious awning one could traverse the valley of the Mystic—green meadows, fields riotous with blossomed clover, fragrant orchards and quaint old farmhouses...passing under bridges, over rivers, between high embankments and through deep cuttings." The tow-path became a favorite place to promenade.[2]

Living in their house near the Cradock Bridge, Sarah Lloyd and Nathan Wait had become well-established members of the community. In 1800 Nathan was one of three men appointed clerk of the market to oversee the ever-increasing business in the market square. That same year his two oldest daughters, Sarah and Harriet, were enrolled in Medford's prestigious "school for young ladies" run by Mrs. Susanna Rowson.[3]

On April 29, 1807 Pastor Osgood noted in his diary that he had met with Nathan Wait. The next Sunday, May 3, all six of the Wait children were baptized. The decision probably had as much to do with the family's standing in the community as it did with any religious revelation. The youngest, Nathan William, was seven years old. The oldest, Sarah Lloyd, was by then twenty-one years old, married, and had a child of her own who was also baptized that day.[4,5] By 1808 Nathan's status was such that he was elected one of the town selectmen, a position he held several years. In 1810 he was elected constable and, according to the date on his fire bucket (now displayed at the Royall House), was invited to join the Medford Amicable Fire Department that same year.[6] During that time he also bought several pieces of property—most notably, the property that had first been home to Sarah and John and their family and had become home to his own family.

There is an intriguing story about Nathan included in Charles Brooks' *History of the Town of Medford* in which Brooks claims for Nathan Wait the honor of being the first person in the United States to have rescued a fugitive slave. Slavery had been against the law in Massachusetts since 1790. The Constitution of the Commonwealth of Massachusetts, by virtue of its first article declaring "all men free and equal," had served to outlaw slavery. A few suits were brought early on by slaves against their masters and the court decisions made it clear that the first article, declaring "all men free and equal," applied to both black and white. "One of Colonel Isaac Royall's slaves, named Belinda, after fifty years of servitude petitioned the General Court in 1783 for an allowance out of the estate of said Royall for herself and her infirm daughter, and the Court 'on the petition of Belinda, the African, Resolved, that she be paid out of the...estate of the late Isaac Royall.'"[7]

In about 1810, a southern plantation owner, the son of a Captain Ingraham who lived in Medford, came to Medford to visit his father and brought his slave, Caesar, with him. Caesar had been a slave in Massachusetts years earlier and was known to some of the people of Medford. Back again in Medford, Caesar came to understand that he could be a free man in Massachusetts. "He accordingly attempted to escape from his master. But, not having laid his plan with sufficient skill, he was overtaken in the upper part of the town, on his way to Woburn, and closely buckled into a chaise by Mr. Ingraham, who intended to drive into Boston with him, and lodge him on board the vessel which was to convey both of them home. Caesar, however, had a trusty friend in Mr. Nathan Wait, the blacksmith, who had promised in no extremity to desert him; and as the chaise reached Medford Bridge, upon the edge of which stood Mr. Wait's smithy, he roared so lustily that Mr. Wait sprang out of his shop, hot from the anvil, and, standing before the horse, sternly forbade the driver from carrying a free man into slavery. Being ordered to mind his own business, he indignantly shook his fist at Mr. Ingraham, and retorted, that he would hear from him again in a manner less acceptable. A general commotion then ensued among Caesar's friends, and they included many of the most respectable citizens in the whole town. Apprehensions were entertained that he would be secreted, and that his pursuers might be subjected to a long, and perhaps fruitless, search. In those days, one daily coach maintained the chief intercourse between Boston and Medford. Accordingly, on the evening of this memorable day, Mr. Ingraham was one of the passengers who happened to be returning to Medford. His unguarded whisper to his next neighbor, 'I have him safe now on shipboard,' chanced to be over heard by some ladies, who speeded the intelligence to Caesar's friends. Their course then became clear. Mr. Wait instantly obtained from the Governor of the State the requisite authority and officers, proceeded to the vessel, and brought off Caesar in triumph."[8]

Was Sarah perhaps one of the women on the coach that night? There is no record of who reported what they had overheard to Nathan, because the coach driver had "a convenient shortness of memory, which wholly disqualified him from recollecting who were his female passengers that evening."[9] In the later years of her life Sarah would have made many trips between Medford and Boston, and so perhaps she was on the coach that night. Most of her family had their homes in Boston, and in the years after John's death she must have often visited her mother who was by then living with her brother Nathaniel in the house on Hollis Street. Mary died on May 20, 1796, "in the front chamber" of that house.[10] A poem, *A Few Lines Occasioned by the Much-Lamented Death of Mrs. Mary Bradlee, who departed this Life, May 20, 1796*, is printed in the Bradlee genealogy, but it is a generic lament which tells nothing about Sarah's mother.

After her mother's death Sarah would have gone to Boston frequently to see her children and grandchildren. One of these visits was recounted many years later by Sarah's then ninety-two-year-old grandson, John Andrews Fulton. Sarah was at her son Samuel's house when five-year-old John Andrews came running home, frightened by a gander that had chased him across the Boston Common. Sarah's response was to "put a good stout stick in his hand, give him pat on the back and send him back to the scene of his discomfiture with the words, 'Always face your enemies, John.'"[11]

Pastor Osgood died in 1822. As in so many churches in New England, the controversies that had been festering in the New England churches throughout Sarah's lifetime finally forced a split in the Medford church. The growing theological division between the orthodox and liberal congregations had been masked during the Revolutionary years by their united support for the patriot cause. But since the time of the Great Awakening many of the churches, particularly those in Boston and its environs, had been redefining their theology. "They rejected as unbiblical the traditionally held Calvinist doctrines of original sin, total depravity, predestination and the trinity. They adopted positive doctrines of the nature of humanity and the possibility of continuing moral, spiritual, and intellectual growth."[12] They came to be labeled Unitarians, even though the rejection of the concept of the Trinity was only one part of their evolving theology.

When Osgood had begun his ministry in Medford in 1774 his ordination had been opposed by a few members who could not support his strict Calvinist views. In the ensuing years most of the townspeople had gradually come to reject the Calvinist doctrine in favor of Unitarian beliefs. At Osgood's death the congregation chose Andrew Bigelow, a Harvard graduate and an unabashed Unitarian, as their new minister. Among the clergy invited to install the new pastor was John Kirkland, minister at New South from 1794 to 1810 and then president of Harvard.[13] Those of the congregation who could not subscribe to the liberal religion broke away and formed the Second, or Trinitarian, Parish.[14] Sarah remained part of the First Parish.

Since the beginnings of the Massachusetts Bay Colony the town and the parish had been a single entity. The meeting house had been the physical embodiment of the Puritan vision of a community in which religious and civic life were inseparable. By the beginning of the nineteenth century, in Medford, as in towns all over New England, it had been formally recognized that that unity no longer existed. The meeting house would no longer serve as the town hall, and town taxes would no longer be used to support the church.[15]

In 1824 the Marquis de Lafayette again returned to the United States, still much revered by the American people. He toured the United States for more than a year, greeted by great crowds in every city. Following huge celebrations in Boston, Lafayette came to Medford on August 28 as a guest of John Brooks who had just finished two terms as the governor of Massachusetts. The whole town (18,000) turned out to greet him, with some of Sarah's great grandchildren surely among the school children lined up along the road. Lafayette then stood at the door of the Brooks house while the townspeople filed past to meet him. The newspaper account of the day recounts, "the main streets and the houses which he passed were filled with children and people, who expressed their gratitude and joy on beholding the man who had done so much for their country. A company of artillery fired a salute, arches were thrown across the street decorated with flags and flowers and evergreens."[16]

That evening, as the governor and the marquis and several privileged guests were dining, Sarah's grandniece Mary Eaton says that "Mrs. Fulton, then an old lady, walked to the governor's house in Medford and inquired for Lafayette. He was at dinner, so she waited a short time, and getting impatient, walked into the dining room and accosted General Lafayette. He recognized her at once, remembering her from his visit to her house, which he made accompanied by her brother David."[17] Their conversation must have included reminiscences of David, who had died unexpectedly thirteen years prior.

Eliza Gill paints a somewhat more dignified picture of Sarah's encounter with Lafayette in her depiction of the marquis' visit, recounting, "he called on our Revolutionary heroine, Mrs. John Fulton (born Sarah Bradlee). At this time he presented her with a breast-pin, now in possession of descendants of hers (Rindge family) in Cambridge."[18] Even then, near the end of her long life, Sarah was still remembered as a brave and determined patriot, and was again honored for her courage by one of the heroes of the Revolutionary War.

Sarah Bradlee Fulton spent her last years living on the farm with her two unmarried daughters, Ann Wier and Elizabeth Scott. "She saw grandchildren and great-grandchildren grow up around her, and in the atmosphere of their love and reverence she spent her last days."[19] "Her humble home was always hospitably open, especially to the children of her brothers, who, if they could leave the luxury of their own homes and come to Medford for a visit, their happiness was complete."[20]

"In spite of the long distance, Sarah Fulton, even in extreme old age, was in the habit of walking to and from the Unitarian Church every Sunday. Those who knew her could scarcely comprehend that she had passed four-score years and ten."[21]

"One gray November morning, "the 'Passing Bell' announced that a life was ended. Seventy, eighty, ninety, ninety-five, the bell tolled out, and many guessed that the aged mistress of the woodland farm, who only the day before had been about her usual tasks, was gone. A procession came slowly through the gate of the burying-place. There walked sons and daughters, grandchildren and great-grandchildren, but the old friends who had known Sarah Fulton in her youth were gathered there before her in their narrow homes."[22]

AFTERWORD

Sarah died November 9, 1835, little more than a month short of her ninety-fifth birthday, and was buried in the Salem Street Cemetery in Medford, in the Wait family tomb.

At the first town meeting after Sarah's death, the old road to Stoneham, where she had lived for fifty years, was renamed Fulton Street in her honor.[1]

Sixty-five years later, on May 26, 1900, the Sarah Bradlee Fulton chapter of the DAR gave her a grave marker—a granite stone that had been her doorstep at the house on Fulton Street[2]—on which was inscribed *Sarah Bradlee Fulton, 1740-1835, A Heroine of the Revolution.* The stone had been a gift from Gen. S. C. Lawrence, the first mayor of Medford, and the present owner of the Fulton property.[3]

Among those present at the ceremony were two who had also attended her burial sixty-five years before: Mrs. Susan Smith Wait, widow of Sarah's grandson Nathan W. Wait, and their son, Francis A. Wait.[4] My grandmother, Ellen Louise Adams Tisdale, and my great aunt, Fanny Fulton Adams, were there, too.[5] As a young woman living in Medford, my mother put flowers on the grave each Memorial Day.

Sarah was the first of six generations of Medford women for whom the Medford First Parish was part of their lives. My mother never relinquished her membership in this church. Immediately after the Second World War, when I was four years old, my parents took my sister and me on the train from California to meet our grandparents and to have us dedicated at the Medford First Parish.

That the stories of Sarah Bradlee Fulton's deeds have been preserved is due in large part to the founding members of the Medford Historical Society (1896) and the Sarah Bradlee Fulton Chapter of the DAR (1897). Most notable were Helen Tilden Wild and Eliza Gill, the authors of many of the articles that appeared in the Historical Society's publication, *The Medford Historical Register*. Their writings in the early issues of the *Register* recount the stories about Sarah that my mother told me when I was a child.

The first president of the Medford Historical Society was William Cushing Wait, a great-great grandson of Sarah Bradlee Fulton. Three of the other founding members were Sarah's great grandchildren, Francis, Hetty, and Sarah Wait. Their mother, Susan Smith Wait, had married Sarah's grandson, Nathan W. Wait in 1829 and the children had grown up in a house on Main Street just a few steps away from the house where Sarah and John had lived during the Revolution. Susan would have known Sarah well, and Susan's son, Francis, born in 1829, would have had some memory of her. For all of them, the stories about Sarah would have been part of the fabric of who they were. Susan Smith Wait (1805-1902) and John Andrews Fulton (1806-1900), Sarah's grandson through Samuel Bradlee Fulton, were honored guests at some of the early DAR chapter meetings where they recounted their tales of Sarah. How I wish I had a transcript of those gatherings.

NOTES

MHR = Medford Historical Register, Medford, Massachusetts

NEHGS = New England Historic Genealogical Society, Boston, Massachusetts

MHS = Massachusetts Historical Society, Boston Massachusetts

FOREWORD

1. Wild, Helen T., *The Royall House Loan Exhibition*, MHR Vol. 2, 1899, p. 123.

THE DRESS

1. Britton-Warren, Claire, email of 6/16/2003 describing her meeting with Alden O'Brien, Curator of Costumes and Textiles at the DAR Museum in Washington, D.C.

2. O'Brien, Alden, email of 9/16/2009 describing the dress.

3. O'Brien email.

4. Britton-Warren email.

5. Records of the Arlington Street Church in Boston, NEHGS website – Boston Church Records, p. 67.

6. ------, pp. 12 and 53.

7. Both John and his brother/cousin, Robert, are identified as distillers in various documents. In the Selectmen's Minutes of 1737 a John Fulton, of Essex Street, is recorded having been disallowed of a license to be a retailer of "strong drink" (Boston Selectmen 1736-1742). At his death in 1760 his wife, Ann Wyer, and his son, Robert, inherited his property on Essex Street (Fulton Genealogy). I am bothered by the fact that our John Fulton is apparently not included in this document, but Ann Wyer must have been his mother. Firstly, John and Sarah named their second daughter Ann Weir, and, as almost all parents of the time, they clearly named their children after parents,

grandparents, and great-grandparents. Secondly, Brooks' *History of the Town of Medford* states that SBF's mother "was a Wier, who came over with the Scotch-Irish" company (p. 506). It is obviously a mistake to name Ann as Sarah's mother rather than John's, but it clearly links Ann to John.

8. Thwing, Annie Haven, *Inhabitants and Estates of the Town of Boston 1630-1800*, CD-ROM, NEHGS, REFCODE 20430.

9. Drake, Samuel Adams, *Old Landmarks and Historic Personages of Boston*, Little, Brown and Company, Boston, 1906, p. 406.

PURITAN ANCESTORS

1. Fisher, David Hackett, *Albion's Seed, Four British Folkways in America*, Oxford University Press, New York, Oxford, 1989, p. 189.

2. ------, p. 163.

3. Wright, Conrad, *Congregational Polity, A Historical Survey of Unitarianism and Universalist Practice*, Skinner House Books, Boston, 1997, pp. 7-8.

4. Wesley, Alice Blair, Peter Hughes and Frank Carpenter, "The Unitarian Controversy and Its Puritan Roots," posted October 13, 2000, in the *Dictionary of Unitarian and Universalist Biography*, an online resource of the Unitarian Universalist History and Heritage Society.

5. Fisher, *Albion's Seed*, p. 31.

6. Morgan, Edmund S., *Visible Saints, The History of a Puritan Idea*, New York University, New York, 1963, pp. 63, 100-1.

7. ------, p. 88.

8. Walker, Williston, *Ten New England Leaders*, Silver, Burdett and Company, New York, Boston, Chicago, 1901, pp. 111-112.

9. *The Great Migration*, NEHGS website, p. 59.

10. Dorchester Town Records, Fourth Report of the Record Commissioners of the City of Boston, Document 9 - 1880, Boston, Rockwell and Churchill, City Printers, No. 39 Arch Street, 1880, p. 8.

11. ------, p. 13.

12. ------, p. 31.

13. Orcutt, William Dana, *Good Old Dorchester, a Narrative History of the Town, 1630-1893*, John Wilson and Son, University Press, Cambridge, 1893, p. 293.

14. *History of the Town of Dorchester, Massachusetts, by a committee of the Dorchester Antiquarian and Historical Society*, Boston: Ebenezer Clapp, Jr., 184 Washington Street, 1851 to 1859, p. 420.

15. Monaghan, E. Jennifer, *Learning to Read and Write in Colonial America*, University of Massachusetts Press, Amherst and Boston, 2007, p. 41.

16. *History of the Town of Dorchester*, p. 117.

17. ------, p. 101.

18. Records of the First Church at Dorchester in New England 1636-1734, George H. Ellis, 141 Franklin Street, Boston, 1891, p. 6.

19. *History of the Town of Dorchester*, p. 209.

20. ------, p. 226; Dorchester Town Records, Fourth Report, p. 196.

21. Dorchester Town Records, Fourth Report, p. 196.

22. *History of the Town of Dorchester*, pp. 238-9; Dorchester Town Records, Fourth Report, p. 236.

23. *History of the Town of Dorchester*, p. 230; Dorchester Town Records, Fourth Report, p. 228.

24. Fisher, *Albion's Seed*, p. 118.

25. ------, p. 140.

26. Orcutt, pp. 50-1.

27. ------, p. 219.

28. Records of the First Church at Dorchester in New England, pp. 243-50.

29. Fisher, *Albion's Seed*, p. 120.

30. ------, p. 121.

31. ------, p. 122.

32. ------, p. 122.

33. Morgan, pp. 126-8.

34. ------, pp. 131-2.

CHILDHOOD

1. Massachusetts Vital Records to 1850, Records Relating to the Early History of Boston, A Report of the Record Commissioners, Document 59, 1890, Dorchester, Volume 1, p. 95, NEHGS website.

2. Orcutt, p. 115.

3. Doggett, Samuel Bradlee, *History of the Bradley Family: With Particular Reference to the Descendants of Nathan Bradley, of Dorchester, Massachusetts,* Press of Rockwell and Churchill, Boston, 1878, p. 12.

4. Orcutt, pp. 119-120.

5.*Colonial Soldiers and Officers in New England, 1620-1775, Massachusetts Soldiers in the French and Indian Wars, 1744-1755,* NEHGS website.

6.Franklin, Benjamin, *The Autobiography of Benjamin Franklin,* American Book Co., New York, 1896, p. 121.

7.*History of the Town of Dorchester,* pp. 303-4.

8.------, p. 305.

9.------, p. 312.

10.Wright, Conrad, *A Stream of Light, A Short History of American Unitarianism,* Skinner House Books, Boston, 1975, pp. xii-xiii.

BOSTON BEFORE THE WAR

1.Doggett, p.10.

2. ------, p. 12.

3.Records Relating to the Early History of Boston, A Report of the Record Commissioners, Document 88, Boston Town Records, 1760, p. 33, www.archive.org.

4.Thwing, *Inhabitants,* REFCODE 6833

5.Burnaby, Rev. Andrew, *Travels through the Middle Settlements in North-America in the Years 1759 & 1760,* T. Payne, London, 1775, pp. 77-78.

6.Chandler, Alfred D., Editor, *A Nation Transformed by Information,* Oxford University Press, New York, 2000. p. 5.

7.Bell, J. L., Boston 1775 Blog, 10/6/2009, Boston's Town Criers and Lost Boys.

8.Thwing, Annie Haven, *The Crooked and Narrow Streets of the Town of Boston 1630-1822,* Marshall Jones Company, Boston, 1920, p. 152.

9. *The Diary of John Rowe 1764-1779*, John Wilson and Son, Cambridge, 1895, p. 14, www.archive.org.

10. Drake, p. 396.

11. Bacon, Edwin M., *Rambles around Old Boston*, Little, Brown and Company, Boston, 1914, p. 14.

12. Records Relating to the Early History of Boston, A Report of the Records Commissioners, Document 55, Boston Town Records 1764-1768, p. 304, www.archive.org.

13. Records Relating to the Early History of Boston containing Miscellaneous Papers, Registry Department of the City of Boston, Document 100, p. 318, www.archive.org.

14. Monaghan, p. 276.

15. ------, p. 293.

16. ------, p. 277

17. *A Receipt in Full*, MHR Vol. 20, 1917, p. 18.

18. Thwing, p. 180.

19. ------, p. 181.

20. Drake, Francis Samuel, *Life and Correspondence of Henry Knox*, Samuel G. Drake, Boston, 1873, pp. 8-9.

21. Drake, Samuel Adams, *Old Landmarks*, p. 380.

22. Obituary, *Boston Evening Post*, December 11, 1769, MHS Annotated Newspapers of Harbottle Dorr, Jr., www.masshist.org.

23. Records of the New South Church in Boston, NEHGS website – Boston Church Records, p. 38.

24. ------, p. 40.

25. Cooke, George Willis, *Unitarianism in America*, American Unitarian Association, Boston, 1910, p. 53.

EARLY YEARS OF MARRIAGE

1. Records Relating to the early History of Boston, A Report of the Records Commissioners, Document 55, Boston Selectmen's Records 1764-1768, p. 6. www.archive.org.

2. Doggett, p. 18; Records of the New South Church in Boston, p. 45.

3. Doggett, pp. 18-19; Records of the New South Church in Boston, pp. 46, 48, 50, 53.

4. Letter of Thomas Bradlee (son of Sarah's brother Nathaniel) of June 11, 1859, relating to his membership in NEHGS, paper files of NEHGS.

5. Monaghan, pp. 314-16.

THE LIBERTY TREE

1. Fisher, David Hackett, *Liberty and Freedom*, Oxford University Press, New York, 2005, pp. 19-21

2. ------, p. 22

3. ------, p. 22

4. Archer, Richard, *As If an Enemy's Country*, Oxford University Press, New York, 2010, p. 30.

5. www.ancestry.com

6. Archer, pp. 35-6.

7. ------, pp. 36-7.

8. ------, p. 68.

9.Masthead, *The Boston-Gazette and Country Journal*, November 2, 1767, MHS Annotated Newspapers of Harbottle Dorr, Jr., www.masshist.org.

10.Archer, pp. 76-81.

11.------, pp. 85-8.

THE OCCUPIED CITY

1.Records Relating to the early History of Boston, A Report of the Records Commissioners, Document 55, Boston Selectmen's Records 1764-1768, 8/4/1768, p. 304. www.archive.org.

2.Records Relating to the Early History of Boston, A Report of the Records Commissioners, Document 42, Boston Selectmen's Minutes, 1769, 8/16/1769, p. 29. www.archive.org

3.Doggett, p. 12.

4.NEHGS website, *Old Cemeteries of Boston*, p. 542.

5.Bell, *Boston 1775*, 2/26/2007, The Funeral of Christopher Seider.

6.Archer, pp. 178-81.

7.Thwing, *Inhabitants*, REFCODE 18704.

8.Drake, Samuel Adams, *Old Landmarks*, pp. 274-5.

9.Eaton, Mary Allen (granddaughter of Sarah's sister, Margaret Lord Fulton Eaton), letter published in the *Boston Transcript*, Saturday, December 21, 1889.

MEDFORD

1. Records of the New South Church in Boston, p. 53.

2.Brooks, Charles, *History of the Town of Medford, Middlesex County, Massachusetts, from Its First Settlement in 1630 to 1855*, Rand, Avery and Company, Boston, 1886, p. 85.

3.------, p. 410

4. Hooper, John H., *Proceedings of the Celebration of the 275th Anniversary of the Settlement of Medford, Massachusetts*, Medford, 1905, pp. 31-2.

5. Gleason, Hall, *Old Ships and Ship-building Days*, MHR Vol. 26, p. 64.

6. Wild, Helen, *The Royall House Loan Exhibition*, MHR Vol. 2, p. 119.

7. Wild, Helen, *A Business Man of Long Ago*, MHR Vol. 3, pp. 88-89. This article discusses the eventual purchase of the property by Sarah's daughter and son-in-law.

8. Hooper, John, *The Taverns of Medford*, MHR Vol. 8, p. 11. This article also discusses the ownership of the property by Isaac Royall

9. Goodwin, R. J. P., *The Medford Blacksmith*, MHR Vol. 1, p. 16.

10. Wild, *A Business Man*, pp. 77-8.

11. Coolidge, Ruth Dame, *Round About Old Medford*, Medford Historical Society, 1934, p. 9.

12. Gleason, pp. 64-5.

13. *Sibley's Harvard Graduates*, Vol. 17, p. 570, University of Michigan General Digital Collection.

14. Brooks, p. 238.

15. Bacon, Edwin, *Washington Street*, Macullar Parker Company, Boston, 1913, no page numbers.

THE TEA PARTY

1. Eaton, Boston Transcript letter.

2. Records Relating to the Early History of Boston, Document 55, Boston Selectmen's Minutes, 1768, p. 307 and Document 42, 1773, p. 186, www.archive.org.

3. Carp, Benjamin L., *Defiance of the Patriots, The Boston Tea Party and the Making of America*, Yale University Press, New Haven and London, 2011, pp. 13-14.

4. ------, pp. 2-3.

5. ------, pp. 81-2.

6. Drake, Francis Samuel, *Tea Leaves*, A. O. Crane, Boston, 1884, p. LIV.

7. ------, p. XCVI-XCVII.

8. Eaton, Boston Transcript letter.

9. Drake, *Tea Leaves*, p. CX.

10. ------, p. LXV.

11. ------, p. XCVI.

12. ------, p. LXV.

13. ------, p. XCVII.

14. Carp, p. 142.

15. Drake, *Tea Leaves*, p. XCVI.

16. Wild, Helen T., *Medford in the Revolution, Military History of Medford, Massachusetts, 1765-1783*, J. C. Miller, Medford, 1903, p. 5.

17. ------, p. 6.

18. Wild, *A Business Man*, p. 81.

THE WAR BEGINS

1. Everett, Edward, *Life of John Stark, in The Library of American Biography, Volume I, conducted by Jared Sparks*, New York, Harper and Brothers, 1856, p. 56.

2. Philbrick, Nathaniel, *Bunker Hill, A City, A Siege, A Revolution*, Viking, New York, 2013, pp. 211-12.

3. Sons of the American Revolution membership application of Francis B. C. Bradlee, 1927.

4. Philbrick, pp. 197-8.

5. ------, p. 202.

6. Ketchum, Richard M., *Decisive Day, The Battle for Bunker Hill*, Henry Holt and Company, New York, 1962, p. 135.

7. Memoirs of Deceased Members of the NEHGS, Frederick Wainwright Bradlee, New England Historic and Genealogical Register, 1929, Vol. 83, p. 111.

8. Wild, *Medford in the War of the Revolution*, MHR Vol. 2, p. 35.

9. Philbrick, p. 220.

10. Wild, *Medford in the War of the Revolution*, MHR Vol. 2, p. 35.

11. Wild, *The Royall House Loan Exhibition*, MHR Vol. 2, 1899, p. 120.

12. Goodwin, R. J. P., *The Medford Blacksmith*, MHR Vol. 1, p. 18.

13. Coolidge, Ruth Dame, *Simon Tufts the Third, Merchant of India*, MHR Vol. 41, p. 34.

14. Wild, Helen T., *Sarah Bradlee Fulton*, MHR Vol. 1, p. 54.

15. Philbrick, p. 230.

16. Medford Tax Records, Vol. 3, 1735-1777, p. 221. www.ancestry.com

17. Brooks, p. 348.

18. Daughters of the American Revolution membership application of descendant of Frances Burns Fulton and Thomas Tilden.

19. Wild, *Medford in the War of the Revolution*, MHR Vol. 2, p. 37.

20. Wild, *Sarah Bradlee Fulton*, MHR Vol. 1, p. 54.

21. ------, p. 55.

22. Coolidge, Ruth Dame, *Medford and George Washington*, MHR Vol. 34, pp. 57-65.

23. Wild, *Sarah Bradlee Fulton*, p. 55.

24. Oral history: my mother always included this in her story. I have never read it anywhere.

25. Philbrick, p. 197.

26. Wild, *Sarah Bradlee Fulton*, p. 55; Eaton, Boston Transcript letter.

27. Wheildon, William Willder, *Siege and Evacuation of Boston and Charlestown*, Lee & Shepard, Boston, 1876, p. 37. "On the 16th of February ... The river and bays were still frozen."

28. Brooks, p. 135.

29. Wild, *Medford in the Revolution*, p. 15.

30. Philbrick, p. 286. From James Thatcher's A Military Journal of the American Revolution.

31. Wild, *Medford in the War of the Revolution*, MHR Vol. 2, p. 38.

THE WAR MOVES ON

1.Wild, *Medford in the Revolution*, p. 18.

2.------, pp. 15-6, p. 58.

3.Wild, *A Business Man*, p. 81.

4.Commager, Henry Steele, and Richard B. Morris, editors, *The Spirit of 'Seventy-Six, The Story of the American Revolution*, Harper & Rowe, New York, 1958, p. 152.

5.Wild, *Medford in the Revolution*, p. 25.

6.------, p. 20

7.Brooks, p. 136.

8.Commager, p. 649.

9.Osgood, David, *Reflections on the Goodness of God...*, T and J Fleet, Boston, 1784, p. 11, Eighteenth Century Collections Online, Print Editions (ECCO).

10.Brooks, p. 501.

11.Osgood, p. 13.

12.Wild, *A Business Man*, p. 83.

13.Gleason, Hall, *Captain Isaac Hall*, MHR Vol. 8, p. 102.

14.Gleason, Hall, *Old Ships and Ship-building Days*, MHR Vol. 26, pp. 65-6.

THE FARM ON THE ROAD TO STONEHAM

1.Deed recorded January 12, 1793 in Middlesex Deeds, Cambridge Court House.

2. Brooks, p. 23.

3.Doggett, p. 18.

4. Records of the New South Church, pp. 59 and 61.

5. Doggett, p. 19.

6. Eaton, Mary Allen.

7. The Lodge of St. Andrews and the Massachusetts Grand Lodge, Boston, 1870, p. 234. www.archive.org

8. *Mystic River above the Bridge, 1835-1850*, MHR Vol. 6, p. 18.

9. Wild, *A Business Man*, pp. 88-89.

10. *The Great Fire in Medford*, MHR Vol. 6, p. 66.

11. *Afoot Through the Fells*, MHR Sept-Dec. 1935, p. 61.

12. Gill, Eliza, *Report of the Jan. 3, 1898 meeting of the SBF Chapter*, American Monthly Magazine, Vol. 12, pp. 289-290.

THE NEW COUNTRY

1. Maier, Pauline, *Ratification*, Simon and Schuster, New York, 2010, p. 30.

2. ------, p. 144.

3. Brooks, p. 138.

4. Maier, p. 155.

5. ------, p. 166.

6. ------, pp. 166-7.

7. ------, p. 207.

8. *Diary of David Osgood*, Oct. 29, 1789, Medford Public Library.

9. *Unpublished Manuscript*, MHR Vol. 11, pp. 94-5.

10. *The Quincy Evening News*, March 13, 1931, Newspaper article about Alice E. Fulton.

11. Wild, *The Royall House Loan Exhibition*, p. 122

12. Wild, Helen T., *Sarah Bradlee Fulton*, MHR Vol. 1, p. 55.

13. *Quincy Evening News*.

14. Sheary, Patrick, Curator of Furnishings at the DAR Museum in Washington, D.C., email of 2/7/11.

15. Vital Records of Medford Massachusetts to the Year 1850, p. 375.

16. *A Receipt in Full*, MHR Vol. 20, p. 19

17. Widows Revolutionary War Pension Application File of Polly Johnston, *#W14981*, www.ancestry.com

18. Medford Selectmen's Order Book 1735 to 1803, www.ancestry.com

19. Medford Accounts Receivable and Accounts Payable 1789-1837, and Medford Selectmen's Records 1807-1816, p. 32, www.ancestry.com

20. Polly Johnston File.

21. Brooks, p. 171.

MEDFORD IN THE NEW CENTURY

1. Brooks, p. 426.

2. Dame, Lorin L., *The Middlesex Canal*, MHR Vol. 1, p. 45.

3. Nason, Elias, *A Memoir of Mrs. Susanna Rowson*, Joel Munsell, Albany, NY, 1870, p. 206.

4. *Diary of David Osgood*.

5. Vital Records of Medford, pp. 158-9.

6. Brooks, p. 128 and p. 118.

7.*Proceedings of the Celebration of the 275th Anniversary*, p. 43.

8.Brooks, pp. 356-7.

9.---------, p. 357.

10.Letter of Thomas Bradlee relating to his membership in NEHGS.

11.Alice Fulton article, *Quincy Evening News*.

12.Wesley, *The Unitarian Controversy*.

13.Brooks, p. 247.

14.------, p. 245.

15.------, p. 251.

16.Gill, Eliza, *Lafayette's Visit to Medford*, MHR Vol. 19, p. 4.

17.Eaton letter.

18.Gill, *Lafayette's Visit to Medford*, p. 5.

19.Wild, *Sarah Bradlee Fulton*, p. 56.

20.------.

21.------.

22.Wild, Helen T., *Dedication of Memorial Tablet to Sarah Bradlee Fulton*, MHR Vol. 3, p. 125.

AFTERWORD

1. Medford Town Records, 1829-1841, Volume 6, Town Meeting March 1836, p. 192. www.ancestry.com

2.Wild, *Dedication of Memorial Tablet*, p. 126.

3.*The Spirit of '76*, Sons of the American Revolution Magazine, March, 1900, p. 123.

4. Wild, *Dedication of Memorial Tablet*, p. 126.

5. DAR Magazine, Vol. 17, Aug. 1900, p. 165.

PHOTOGRAPHS

Nathaniel Bradlee's house in Boston where Sarah helped disguise her husband and brothers for the "Tea Party." Picture used by permission of the Royall House and Slave Quarters.

Plaque marking the site of Sarah's first home in Medford.

Sarah's house on the Road to Stoneham. The picture is framed in wood taken from a shutter in Nathaniel Bradlee's house. Picture used by permission of the Royall House and Slave Quarters.

Sarah's house on the Road to Stoneham. Picture used by permission of the Royall House and Slave Quarters.

Children's chairs given to Sarah by President George Washington. Beside them is Nathan Wait's fire bucket. Picture used by permission of the Royall House and Slave Quarters

Chinese porcelain dish belonging to Sarah.

A dress belonging to Sarah. Picture used by permission of the Royall House and Slave Quarters.

Ellen Louise Adams Tisdale wearing the dress of her great-great-grandmother, Revolutionary War heroine Sarah Bradlee Fulton (est. 1899). The dress is now housed in the DAR Museum, Washington DC. Photo courtesy of Claire Warren.

Depiction of the dedication of Sarah's grave marker by the Sarah Bradlee Fulton Chapter of the DAR. Picture used by permission of the Royall House and Slave Quarters.

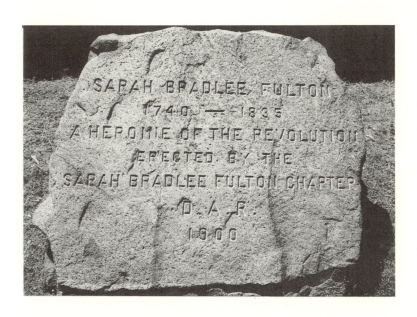

Sarah's grave marker, Salem Street Burying Ground, Medford, Massachusetts

THANK YOU...

To my niece Claire Britton-Warren, who first urged me to go to see the dress and kindly shared her research on Sarah with me. To Alden O'Brien, Curator of Costumes and Textiles at the DAR Museum, who provided the history of the dress, and to the DAR Museum for allowing me to use the photograph of the dress. To Medford historian Dee Morris, who critiqued my manuscript and gave me such enthusiastic encouragement on each of my visits to Medford. To Tom Lincoln, Executive Director of the Royall House and Slave Quarters, who spent several hours with me while I looked through the old records of the Sarah Bradlee Fulton Chapter of the DAR. To Molly McGrath of Pink Eraser Editorial Services who, always sensitive to the integrity of my writing, gave me so much valuable editing help.

My family was my constant source of encouragement. My daughter Kate gave me good advice for moving the narrative forward. My daughter-in-law Sarah did the final layout to ready the book for publication. My son Mark and my son-in-law Matt both cheered me on. And I especially thank my husband Jim. He read through many rough drafts and complimented me on every one. He never complained about the hours I spent reading and writing, or about the fact that half the kitchen table was always covered with books. And finally to my grandchildren, Katherine, Grace, Libby, Hannah, Luke, and Olivia who all kept telling me to write my book. I hope you will tell your children about Sarah.